QUESTIONS of the SPIRIT

the quest for understanding at a time of loss

BRENT GREEN

ACCLAIM FOR QUESTIONS OF THE SPIRIT

"Love and loss are two sides of the same coin. Brent Green's deeply insightful book explores both sides with equal rigor, skill and passion. This book is, ultimately, a guide to being fully human. We are mortal beings and Questions of the Spirit shows readers how we can revel in and be enriched by the truth of that mortality."

— DR. BILL THOMAS
Author of *Second Wind: Navigating the Passage to a Slower, Deeper and More Connected Life*

"Brent Green's wonderful book offers us the guidance we need when we lose someone we love. It's the kind of book we want to read before we lose someone we love and afterwards to remind us of the journey we all must go through. You will read it with joy as a reminder of how to keep our hearts open, even in the face of the inevitable losses we all must endure. It is truly a gift of love."

— JED DIAMOND, PH.D.
Author, *Male Menopause, The Enlightened Marriage*, and many more

"Wow! This is Brent Green's sixth and finest work—and right up there with the best books focused on loss, grief and renewal. Calling on his background in counseling psychology, he inspires readers to search within for answers to challenging and unresolved spiritual questions. The depth and flow of the narrative kept me engaged, helping me learn more about myself along the way. Appreciative audiences will benefit from his hard-won wisdom. I give this book five stars!"

— CAROL ORSBORN, PH.D.
Author, *Fierce with Age, The Spirituality of Age, The Art of Resilience*, and many more

"I have savored every page. It is such a beautiful and insightful read. This book will be Brent's legacy, to his family and to our generation. I suppose because I know him, examples using family and friends are especially poignant, but also his historical references to people and events we Baby Boomers have in common. It's almost like reading my own history. It makes the book so meaningful. Truly a tour-de-force!"

— DAWN LEHMAN
Author, *Smart Talk* and Public Speaker, Performer

"Questions of the Spirit is a beautiful and transcendent book for all ages. I was overwhelmed by the feeling of a comforting spiritual presence, which grew as the book plunged deeply into the great existential questions of life. This book is also of crucial importance for the Boomer generation. Always a questioning generation, Boomers have now entered the most spiritual life-stage as they resolve their purpose and meaning and work out their own spirituality. This is precisely the book to help them navigate through these issues and, for many, a lifetime of accumulated grief."

— REV. DR. WILLIAM B. RANDOLPH
Director of Aging and Older Adult Ministries
Discipleship Ministries | The United Methodist Church

"Brent Green is a brilliant writer, and Questions of the Spirit really connected with me. Reading this book after experiencing a personal loss is like having your own support group with you all the time. After losing the love of my life, I'm very grateful for Brent's wisdom."

— ED PITTOCK
Founder, Home Care Standards Bureau
Founder, Society of Certified Senior Advisors

"Ernest Becker wrote, 'Of all things that move man, one of his principle ones is fear of death.' Indeed, denial of death has a huge impact on grief. Questions of the Spirit begins a much-needed process of asking questions that go to the heart of our denial of death and the defense systems that we erect over a lifetime. This thoughtful book provides an existential approach to grief support while honestly exploring our greatest mystery."

— MARK McGANN, M.A., J.D.
Hospice Chaplain
VITAS Healthcare

"This is a beautifully written book about our inexorable experiences with loss as we move through the life course. Brent presents readers with eighteen remarkably poignant stories revealing experiences with loss not only from its common association with the death of a loved one, but loss of identity, opportunity, success, or relationships that make up our human experience. Each chapter is followed by questions for personal reflection or group discussion that will inspire readers to contemplate their own rarely explored beliefs and values."

— DAVID COX
President, Professional Testing

"Questions of the Spirit is a remarkable document and something that has given me many insights. It's hard to put down! I'm not sure in which category of 'friend' I must put Brent — with a great chapter on that subject and many helpful distinctions — but the book brings me closer to him, and I'm grateful for that. Brent is doing something very, very important here and the book is going to be of huge value to people."

— HARRY R. MOODY, PH.D.
Vice President of Academic Affairs, AARP (ret)
Author, *The Five Stages of the Soul* and *Aging: Concepts and Controversies*

"Questions of the Spirit is a profound gift. I was so moved by Brent's story of loss and grief and how he has harnessed that with wisdom, spirit, intellect and compassion to provide others (including me) with messages, questions and paths to travel in answering the almost unanswerable questions. Weaving his personal experience into the text focuses on reality, wisdom and humanity. I am reading the book bit by bit — and it is helpful. And I might add, it's the first piece that I've read that touches my thoughts and feelings. Others that folks have given me when my husband passed away seem one dimensional in comparison."

— HELEN DENNIS
Specialist in Aging, Employment & The New Retirement
www.ProjectRenewment.com

QUESTIONS OF THE SPIRIT

THE QUEST FOR UNDERSTANDING AT A TIME OF LOSS

Brent Green

ISBN: 0692765158
ISBN 13: 9780692765159
Library of Congress Control Number: 2016913093
Brent Green & Associates, Inc., Denver, COLORADO

For Julie, Joel, Becky, and Heidi

My wife died, Heidi's mother died, Brent's sister died and Becky's sister-in-law died. We were together when Julie left us, and yet very alone in what we saw, felt and lost. Four individual journeys in dealing with the profundity of grief.

Brent openly shares his journey in this book. The "Questions" are not answers but rather spiritual streetlights illuminating the journey. Brent's answers form his journey, my answers form mine.

Your answers will form your journey.

— JOEL BETHKE
Husband, Father, Brother-in-Law

All the sorrows of life are bearable if only we can convert them into a story.

— IZAK DINESEN
Author, Out of Africa

TABLE OF CONTENTS

PREFACE

I HAVE LOST many significant persons in my life. The list includes four grandparents, three uncles and three aunts, both of my parents, a niece, two cousins, six in-laws, several close business colleagues, and two very dear friends. Not once did I seek professional, emotional support or grief counseling. After each loss, I did as many people do in my situation: I grieved introspectively, privately, rarely reaching out to others when I could have used some advice or just a steady shoulder. I pushed through the *five stages of grief* mostly on my own, confronting and coping with *denial, anger, bargaining, depression*, and finally *acceptance*. When I needed an outlet for the jolting emotions following these losses, I tapped into my creative instincts and produced something to reflect my existential grief through writing, drawing, and photography.

Then in October 2015 we lost my sister to stage IV lung cancer, leaving me as the final surviving member of my nuclear family. I did not actively seek out grief support when losing Julie; that counseling came to us, and it has made a significant difference.

My sister passed away while receiving care from a professional, for-profit hospice organization called VITAS Healthcare, described as a "pioneer and leader in the hospice movement since 1978 and the nation's largest provider of end-of-life care," with 11,700 staff members helping terminally-ill patients daily. As I examine more fully in the following introductory chapter, Mark McGann, a VITAS chaplain, visited my sister's home a few days before she died. He asked our family members to gather with him around a dining room table near the kitchen. We were sleep-deprived, anxious, and grief-stricken with the raw weight of realization that Julie was close to death.

Mark's calmness and demeanor made us feel immediately at ease, which, I believe, as a former rehabilitation psychologist, is a quality that cannot be taught or academically cultivated. His authenticity and compassion seemed innate. I felt kinship also because he is close to my age.

To begin that first meeting, Mark asked us a profound question then calmly waited for us to sort through our grief and confusion. He asked, "Is there value in suffering?" My innermost pockets of despair began to surface as I listened to my brother-in-law and niece share their feelings and tears. I then shared my answer, and although now I cannot exactly recall what I said, I know my answer came from an uncensored place, stripped of self-consciousness or guardedness. The question cut to the core of that palpable, immediate encounter with dying and death. Mark's question helped us get in touch with our feelings in those final hours before Julie died and provided us with one avenue to start finding answers where sometimes there are no obvious answers.

Why? Why now? Why her? Why not me? What's next?

Mark appeared once again several days later, almost spontaneously within an hour before Julie died, and he created a ritual that we performed bedside. As she began taking her final breaths, the family encircled her body with cut flowers as dazzling as California sunlight filling the backyard patio next to her bedroom.

Julie had been confirmed as a teenager in the Episcopal Church, although she spent most of her adult life searching for spiritual answers and comfort through many diverse sources, from bestselling books to close encounters with world-class writers and intellectuals. She read dozens of popular books about spirituality, often sending me copies as gifts. During the final months of her life, she attended Christian church services through her television, especially appreciating the optimistic messages and ministry of Joel Osteen, a popular American pastor and televangelist whose Sunday morning program attracts seven million viewers and is seen in over 100 countries worldwide. Osteen is known for his readily available smile and "prosperity gospel."

On my request, and in honor of Julie's traditional religious heritage, Mark read from Episcopalian scripture found in the *Book of Common Prayer*:

Into your hands, O merciful Savior, we commend your
servant Julie. Acknowledge, we humbly beseech you, a sheep of
your own fold, a lamb of your own flock, a sinner of your
own redeeming. Receive her into the arms of your mercy,
into the blessed rest of everlasting peace, and into the
glorious company of the saints in light. Amen.
May her soul and the souls of all the departed, through the
mercy of God, rest in peace. Amen.[1]

With the speaking of these ancient words and the circle of fresh cut flowers surrounding Julie's body, I believe each of us found some immediate relief. She was no longer suffering. We were doing the best we could at the moment of her death to send her off and into the great unknown beyond this life. A much more elaborate *Celebration of Life*—a party befitting my theatrical and event-creating sister, to include her extensive and diverse network of friends and family members—would follow several months later.

My brother-in-law, Joel, continued to meet with Mark for periodic grief counseling sessions, and Joel would call me following these encounters, often excited after some emotional and instructive conversations with such an erudite and philosophical chaplain. He also shared Mark's newest questions and the profundity and impact of their timing. I assembled Mark's questions and realized that I wanted to answer them thoughtfully, not only for my mental and spiritual health but for all of us who have lost and will lose again. VITAS did not have grief counseling services available in Denver where I reside. So, I started writing. And writing. And writing. And the result is the book you now behold.

---

1 *Book of Common Prayer*, "Ministration at the Time of Death", A Commendatory Prayer, 465

Mark is an incredible chaplain and grief counselor, and his unassuming, non-threatening way of counseling those who are grieving can lead to deeper emotional catharsis and wisdom. Answering these questions can become a stairway to greater spiritual awareness, a more resilient comportment, renewed faith, and optimism in the face of tragic loss.

To Mark's questions I've added my own, and after each chapter, I've included still more specific questions that can potentially engage the reader with even deeper insights, thought, and contemplation. My goal isn't for you to answer all the questions posed in this book; some questions may not be relevant to your situation. Rather, my objective is for you to discover just a single question, the answer to which settles some of the turmoil, confusion, and grief that may be in your heart right now. If more than one question challenges and then enlivens you, all the better. Some will choose to read this book in a linear manner, from cover to cover, but a *nonlinear reading* may be helpful for others.

Some of the material included in this book does not focus on loss of another person; rather, I explore other kinds of loss such as loss of a friendship with someone still living, loss of status, loss of a job, loss of self-confidence, loss of purpose, loss of skills, and loss of opportunities. Loss comes in many forms throughout life, and sometimes our emotions during these experiences are as wrenching and life-changing as how we feel when losing a spouse or lover to the ultimate finality of death. Loss means pain, but loss also means growth.

James M. Barrie (1860 — 1937) has been respected for generations because of his enduring masterwork exploring the edges of immortality through a charming children's play entitled *Peter Pan, or the Boy Who Wouldn't Grow Up.* In a provocative memoir about his strong-minded mother after her death, the Scottish dramatist sadly and tersely captures a fundamental life lesson about the impact of loss: "We never understand how little we need in this world until we know the loss of it."[2]

---

2 Barrie, James M., from *Margaret Ogilvy*, as quoted on wikiquote.org: https://en.wikiquote.org/wiki/J._M._Barrie

Chaplain Mark suggested to my brother-in-law that we consider for a moment the thousands of centenarians among us—those 100 years of age and older—many of whom are experiencing active and engaged lives even today at such an advanced age. These people have lost family members, friends, colleagues, and spouses. Most have lost physical vitality, and many confront daily challenges from chronic illnesses, sometimes with unrelenting aches and pain. They have also sometimes lost wealth, material possessions, economic security, and employment. They all have lost stature in our youth-obsessed culture. A long life guarantees a life filled with loss along the way. They have learned to cope with grief in its many forms and nevertheless remained resilient.

Research into the personalities of long-lived people discloses some typical qualities. Those who survive into the years beyond 100 are usually outgoing with positive dispositions, not likely to speak ill of others, laugh often, express their emotions, and tend to be conscientious. Aware of their limited life expectancy, many centenarians still make plans even though the future will usually involve additional loss, including a diminishing circle of friends, neighbors, and relatives.[3]

Dr. Carol Orsborn, my colleague and friend for more than a decade, spent a year chronicling her insights about aging beyond age sixty in a creative and inspiring memoir. The author of twelve books on spirituality and human growth, she conceived a list of precepts about spiritual aging, her *11 Spiritual Truths of Aging*. Her sixth truth is apropos for this discussion: "The gift of longevity provides ample opportunity to not only grow old, but to grow whole."[4] Her tenth truth mirrors my unplanned and diffident plunge into the nature and power of loss: "We don't always get to take a leap of faith. Sometimes we are pushed."[5]

3 Doheny, Kathleen, "Personality Secrets to a Long Life," WebMD Health News, May 30, 2012: https://goo.gl/BPPHWT

4 Orsborn, Carol, *Fierce with Age: Chasing God and Squirrels in Brooklyn*, Turner Publishing, Copyright 2013, page 149

5 Ibid, Orsborn, *Fierce with Age*, 149

Those of us who receive the blessing of a long life will also need to understand and manage grief and loss many times throughout our lives. Grief will come again, and again. Loss is a requisite part of the aging process and the human experience. I have been told that each loss of someone or something close to us has different characteristics and subtleties, challenging our fortitude in unprecedented ways, so we're always learning about grief anew when mourning comes to visit once again.

H. Millard Smith, MD, Ph.D. (1922—2015) was a practicing physician for over four decades, and he wrote an accessible and helpful booklet entitled, *At the Bedside of a Dying Loved-One: Comfort for You During the Watch*, which he shared with many patients, colleagues, and friends. Dr. Smith offered cogent insights into dying and loss and recovery from the perspective of a remarkable, humanistic clinician:

> Death will come. This watching experience cannot be but temporary. Grief will follow, and memory will keep alive your loved-one. Offer your great gift of love—going to the door of death with your loved one. Take the gift from the dying—recognition that life is precious, and to be lived with feeling and meaning. The training and experience you received when living with the loved-one can be passed on to the next generation. Death teaches us to go back to our life, willing to be part of humanity, and willing to help another along the way we must go.[6]

I hope this book helps you with your journey toward insight, acceptance, and peace—the heartfelt light of optimism. So please read on.

---

6 Smith, H. Millard, M.D., Ph.D., *At the Bedside of a Dying Loved-One*, Copyright 1995, published by Cumberland Family Practice, Hendersonville, TN

INTRODUCTION

I MARVELED AT a brilliant Woolly Blue Curls shrub. It burst with vibrant colors: white and bluish-purple flowers with verdant, lime-green leaves. Honey bees buzzed around the bush, landing to sip nectar then moving from flower to flower. A majestic monarch butterfly joined the feast; its wings folded closed as if praying. The late October air felt crisp, but a bright sun warmed my face. A hummingbird flitted into view then whisked away when it discovered this human interloper. Several species of birds chirped in nearby trees, and a hawk lazily soared and circled in a thermal updraft high overhead. This break became a perfect moment to reflect on the majesty and beauty of life, a momentary respite from a grim vigil persisting in a ranch house several yards away and within a master bedroom where my sister struggled and gasped for her final breaths.

Julie, my only sibling, had been battling stage IV lung cancer for 45 months with support from some of best medical care providers in the world, at Stanford, where young and committed doctors worked persistently at the leading edge of medical science and art. Julie had been blessed through most of the course of her disease with symptom-manageable living and opportunities to travel and spend time with geographically dispersed family and friends. A trip to Africa with Joel had become the ultimate realization of a travel dream she had harbored since childhood. She had been mostly optimistic that her doctors could control metastasizing cancer with advanced, targeted chemotherapies. One miracle drug called Tarceva had kept her tumors from spreading and even shrinking for almost eighteen months at the beginning of her journey as a cancer patient. Without these miracle pharmaceutical inter-ventions, her survival prognosis would have been less than six months.

But on this bright October day, Julie was in the final stage of dying, her breathing growing shallower. All of us close to her had already spent many hours sitting with her, speaking softly, playing classic rock music that she had loved, and making sure that rotating hospice personnel treated her as their primary priority, which those good people always did. We watched for signs of pain or discomfort, and Heidi, her regis-tered nurse daughter, remained vigilant through nine days that circum-scribed her spiral from full engagement in life until her final hours. She did not speak to any of us during her last week, mostly, we assumed, due to palliative sedation from multiple drugs, doggedly administered. We hoped that she knew we were there and wanted nothing more than to make her journey from life as peaceful and pain-free as possible.

The purple and white flowering bush in front of her house present-ed me with such a vivid contrast: its vibrant, buzzing life, fulfilling the needs of so many insects and birds. Its color and subtle fragrance lifting my heart toward the bright sky above and reassuring me that something more, something beautiful awaited my sister on the other side of life, reminding me in another tangible way that life will go on even as each of us exits the living world. Plants will flower, birds will chirp, bees will gather flower nectar, and monarch butterflies will gently beat their flaw-less wings to float from plant to plant.

Later I would learn more about the meaning of the monarch but-terfly, occasionally referred to as a "symbol of hope." In some spiritual traditions, butterflies can be a sign of someone who is dying as the soul begins to leave the body. Seeing butterflies while losing a loved one can embody a signal from beyond the physical realm. Other religious tra-ditions insist that angels send butterflies to comfort and reassure the bereaved: the soul of our loved one lives on. The Christian religion un-derstands butterflies as a symbol of resurrection.

As challenging as it is to consider noble existence during an average day, this moment in the final hours of my sister's life instructed me to pay attention to details, to remember each passing hour as precious, and to reconsider my faith and doubts in life after life. Some essence of my sister must go on, I thought. Something of my essence must go on also. Life just cannot be short and then over at death.

A monarch butterfly told me so.

Julie and I had already shared life's most profound death experiences together, connected in those events as siblings working to make everything better. Our parents died at the turn of the century within the same 24-hour span of time. Dad's dying process was difficult over five days, following months of attempted rehabilitation from a mild heart attack. When he finally let go of the reins of life, he disappeared into a coma-like state; his breathing rattled, and he did not seem at peace.

Julie once leaned over his bed and spoke to him, saying, "You can go, Daddy. Your work is done here. Everything will be okay."

She comforted me with her durable leadership in those dying moments and her confidence to usher our father away from this life, a genuinely loving gesture. Our tiny mother rested in a twin bed next to Dad, alert and connected to what was happening to her husband of over sixty years. She had been a nursing home patient for several years due to the ravages of Parkinson's disease, but during her husband's final days, she had become alert and communicated as she did when much younger. She rested nearby when Dad took his last breath, a profound and accepting sigh. Julie understood things I could not then comprehend about loss of this magnitude, although she, too, succumbed to the intense grief that comes with the death of a parent.

Julie and I were at a mortuary later that day to make arrangement for a final viewing of our father's remains, a cremation, and eventually an automobile trip to our parents' hometown 600 miles away. As we were busy selecting an urn, I received a call from my wife, Becky, that my mother had collapsed at breakfast just hours following my father's death. We rushed back to the nursing home to find Mom in the final minutes of life, her breathing labored and shallow. Within a matter of an hour, she took her last breath. Again, Julie was both grief-stricken and resolute. She knew what to do in situations like this. Suddenly we would be planning a dual memorial service for Mom and Dad in their hometown where many lifelong friends still resided.

Health magazine published an article about the close and curious proximity of our parents' deaths, entitled "Can you die of a broken heart?" The writer quoted Julie: "There was no way my mother was going to live without her love of a lifetime. She died of a broken heart." The article continued with its examination of the possibility of dying from a broken heart by interviewing Dr. Bill Thomas, a Harvard-trained geriatrician who founded the Eden Alternative, an innovative approach to designing nursing homes that empower residents and develop community. (Ironically, Dr. Thomas and I would become well acquainted several years later.) He validated my sister's nonclinical conclusion: "Dying of a broken heart can begin with the loss of a spouse, a home, or any other meaningful thing in life. It can happen when one is young, but it probably happens more often when one is old, when the losses mount up, when there is some physical frailty to begin with." [7]

The possibility of dying from a broken heart became even more apparent during the final week of 2016. Carrie Fisher, a celebrated *Star Wars* actor best known for her portrayal of Princess Leia Organa, suffered a heart attack and went into cardiac arrest while flying from London to Los Angeles on December 23. Fisher died four days later at age 60, on December 27. The following day, Debbie Reynolds, her mother and revered Hollywood movie icon with a famously pert demeanor, died suddenly at age 84. TIME magazine further examined this sad and shocking phenomenon: "Broken heart syndrome, or stress-induced cardiomyopathy, can be sparked by an 'extremely stressful event,' even among healthy people, according to the American Heart Association. The condition has been tied to depression, mental health issues and heart disease, and can follow emotionally taxing events like the death of a loved one."[8]

---

7 Evans, Karin, "Can you die of a broken heart?", Health, March 2001, pages 78-82
8 Chan, Melissa, "Did Debbie Reynolds die of a broken heart?" TIME magazine, December 29, 2016, published online: https://goo.gl/L3PJxt

I did not completely understand the lethal magnitude of grief during the days following our parents' passing, but Julie was an emotional anchor for me, helping me stay focused on planning and organizing while interjecting our shared losses with insights and humor. Death is not funny, but many nuances of our human condition can be. Julie was incredibly talented at spotting and commenting on the theater of the absurd.

So, I absorbed the beauty of the flowering shrub with purple and white flowers, astonished with the artful complexity of birds, bees, and flowers, but absent my sister … her strength, her wisdom, her leadership as the older sibling—even sometimes my bossy big sister. I not only recognized the objective facts of my impending loss, but I also became starkly aware that I was about to become the last living member of my nuclear family from childhood. I would be next in line to depart this mortal plane, and with my departure the family of four that had lived, worked, played, dined, worshiped, and traveled together during the second half of the 20th century would all be gone. This realization made me feel a sense of existential loneliness that I had never felt before. I am the final crew member of my unique family ship.

Like most siblings facing a similar loss, I thought back to Julie's life story in preparation to write an obituary that would be needed too soon. She had indeed lived a life full of creativity, passion, engagement, and enthusiasm.

She was born on June 4, 1942, in Topeka, Kansas. She attended Topeka High School where she distinguished herself as the head cheerleader and frequent dramatic lead in theatrical plays staged by the school's critically acclaimed drama department. Although she never became a professional actress, she was regarded and beloved by many for her dramatic flair, her gregariousness, and her charming demeanor. She studied at the University of Kansas with emphasis on the dramatic arts. She also became the first runner-up in the Miss Kansas contest, apparently exceeding talents of the title winner that year with her amazing and memorable interpretation of the final soliloquy of Joan of Arc.

Her career included several years working in social services and more than fifteen years as a self-employed esthetician, where she served an extensive network of devoted San Francisco and Bay Area clients who appreciated this beautiful woman's skills at restoring youthful facial beauty, both externally and internally. Because of her personal commitment to serving others, late in life Julie successfully studied to become an emergency medical technician.

Julie was perhaps most appreciated for her avocational work as an event and meeting creative director, supporting annual sales incentive programs for Sequoia Insurance Company. She notably conceived memorable and immersive experiences that transformed ordinary hotel ballrooms at Pebble Beach into themed events such as the set from *Phantom of the Opera* or a Middle Eastern bazaar.

She spent more than two decades riding cutting horses and participating with Joel in cutting horse competitions, a wellspring for many enduring personal friendships among "horse people" and serious rivalries with this very dedicated and competitive woman.

Julie's compassion for others less fortunate found expression through random acts of kindness, whether regular gifts of cash to homeless street people or private donations to charitable organizations. Her abiding love of animals, great and small, included her five cherished cutting horses and two precocious lap dogs.

She survived one more day, and I did everything I could to pay attention to each nuance involved in saying goodbye forever in this life. I worried over her possible discomforts and second-guessed the professionals administering complex medication cocktails. I tried to play exactly the right musical artists that would reach through the fog of her unconsciousness and remind her of some sublime and cherished times in her life. I marveled at the generosity of hospice staff members who never knew my intelligent, beautiful, and gregarious sister—how nevertheless they seemed to love her in those final days and hours before her departure.

The night before Julie died, I succumbed to exhaustion and rested on a giant mattress next to her hospital bed. Both of her demanding lapdogs, Panda and Spencer Tracy, also slept, a certain tension in their presence as if they could sense Julie's forthcoming leave-taking. I dozed off for a few minutes only to be awakened by a soft melody. A gentle and giving hospice nurse leaned over Julie's bed and sang tenderly to her. I surmised that the nurse must be singing a spiritual song, perhaps of African-American origin, soft, heartening, and hopeful. I am so amazed and comforted that a stranger could care as much for a dying patient, to give from her soul in such a compassionate way.

The following afternoon we gathered around Julie's bed. The on-duty nurse had informed us that Julie's breathing had changed, and signs of death had become evident. Tears streamed down my face from a place I could not control, crying neither censored nor shameful. Everyone wept as the time between her breaths expanded beyond a minute. And, finally, just like our father had passed, Julie took one final breath, almost a sigh, as if nonverbally saying, "I can go now. My work is done here. Everything will be okay."

What amazed me then, as it did everyone else in our attending family, was that Julie looked beautiful in her final repose. She had been spared ravaging assaults of cancer that sometimes can hollow out the victim, leaving her emaciated and ghastly in appearance. Julie's dark coloring sheltered her from the pall of death, her face still appeared full and smooth, and she looked at peace. She died with her eyes partly open, the striking emerald color of her irises almost iridescent as if she was then peering into another dimension that we could not see, as if she gazed into the face of infinitude.

Stepping outside again, I leaned over to smell the subtle fragrance of my hopeful bush, listened to flutter and chirping of many tiny birds, admired bees buzzing, and inhaled crisp air to fill my lungs with the breath of life. I was exhausted and thankful.

In *The Tibetan Book of Living and Dying*, Sogyal Rinpoche addressed my deep sense of connection to nature following my sister's death. "When we finally know we are dying, and all other sentient beings are dying with us, we start to have a burning, almost heartbreaking sense of the fragility and preciousness of each moment and each being, and from this can grow a deep, clear, limitless compassion for all beings."[9]

I knew Julie did not want to die, that she had hoped for more years to travel and be with her husband, daughter, son, brother, sister-in-law, grandchildren, and an adoring circle of friends; that she dreamed of more adventures in Africa or other tropical countries she had loved. I understood in another new way that tomorrow is promised to nobody, and even those deserving a long life sometimes aren't granted more time.

The ephemeral moments following Julie's death also stirred up annoyance. How unfair. How incomplete. How unfortunate her timing to get lung cancer, perhaps just a few years before medical science could grant her a wish of even more vital time, possibly demoting lung cancer in women to the manageable status of a chronic disease. I felt astonishment that Julie had joined a long list of grandparents, uncles, aunts, cousins, and her youngest daughter on the other side, the bookend at the other end of life called infinity.

Honored as a memorial speaker at her 50th high school reunion, Julie concluded her profound speech to her former classmates by addressing her eventual loss with the battle for life. "When my time comes to join our departed classmates," she said, "I think I will embrace the phrase from Sojourner Truth in saying, 'I am not going to die. I am going home like a shooting star.'" Those who knew and loved Julie believe that this woman of many passions and high purposes did exactly that.

My thoughts soared into the puffy clouds and essential questions of existence. Will they be there to greet me when I also cross into the great unknown? Will Julie again become a reassuring and knowledgeable guide in my afterlife? Will we experience salvation and resurrection? Can she tease me again? Or piss me off as my one and only, irrepressible and bossy big sister? I would like to see all those people again, those who have passed on, those responsible for my existence as a sentient

---

9 Rinpoche, Sogyal, as quoted by Goodreads.com, https://www.goodreads.com/quotes/497200

being, as well as those who had seats in the front row, participating in my youth, growth, and maturation. It would be insufficient to live beyond the grave but never reconnect with all the individuals who populated my life's story, as if disconnected spirits, ignorant of their earthly relationships. Do we resurrect intact in such a way that Julie is still Julie when I meet her again as a pure spirit? Will Dad be my Dad again, my wise and worldly father who wanted the best for me to a degree greater than most other human beings in my life? Will my gentle mom appear again and inspire transcendental creativity as she inspired me toward the arts during her life?

It seems that life after death would be wholly incomplete if as spirits we never reconnect with the characters who shaped our personalities and perspectives during life, most of all the people we loved. And to my knowledge, nowhere in the scriptures can be found a clear description of heaven that includes family reunions purified by reconciliations. So, I thought, I owe this to Julie: to search for answers, not just through more rigorous religious education but with reflective meditations about the possibilities of spiritual life after physical death. I need to look at loss without blinking first.

My spiritual search cannot be satisfied alone by dogma or received authority from those who believe they understand the Holy Bible and scriptures better than I do. Yes, I want to learn from them as well, but my spiritual search must include understanding science, from the quantum to the cosmos. If God is watching over us, my bent toward science asks me also to seek empirical evidence, even though faith and science may never converge, even as humanity gets closer to understanding and perceiving infinitesimal and infinite qualities of matter, space, and time. Albert Einstein said, "The further the spiritual evolution of mankind advances, the more certain it seems that the path to genuine religiosity does not lie through the fear of life, and the fear of death, and blind faith, but through striving after rational knowledge."[10]

---

10 Einstein, Albert, as quoted on SimpletoRemember.com, Judaism Online: http://www.simpletoremember.com/articles/a/einstein/

I remember when Dad and I enjoyed lunch at a home-cooking restaurant especially talented with old-fashioned fruit pies. As we relished our slices of apple and cherry pie, Dad revealed to me his innermost theological beliefs outside the dictates of the Christian religion he had dutifully and humbly practiced throughout his adult life. He told me that if there is life after death, then our eternal souls must not remain here on the planet that made our lives possible. Our spirits might end up somewhere else in the vast cosmos and a universe stretching beyond the practical understanding of mere mortals. I sat there listening carefully, feeling reverence for his honesty, his doubts, his intellectual hopefulness, recognizing that a rapidly aging father had just revealed feelings he had not shared with anyone else. It was how Dad let me know that he trusted me, that he was not ashamed to be wrong if not right, and that Dad hoped we'd meet again someday long after he had departed from the living world.

So now I turn to the essential questions governing our human liaison with dying, death, loss, and the possibilities for transcendental existence beyond the breathing years.

WHEN I DIE BY JULIE BETHKE

*If you need to weep, cry for whatever separates you
from anyone you love.*

*And when you need me, put your arms around each
other, and give whatever you need to give or receive
from me.*

*I wanted to leave you something … something better
than words or sound.*

*Look for me in the people I've known and loved. And,
if you cannot give me to them, then let me live in your
eyes and touch and not on your minds.*

*You can love me most by letting hands touch hands.
By letting go of anything that makes you unfree to
love each other.*

*Love doesn't die—people do.
So—when all that is left of me is love, give me away
to one another.*

IS THERE VALUE IN SUFFERING?

MARK MCGANN, THE erudite chaplain and grief counselor working for the hospice that took care of Julie, posed this question as our family sat around a dining room table together, our wife-mother-sister-grandmother dying in the master bedroom ten yards away. "Is there value in suffering?" That moment was as raw as life can be, Julie's departure imminent, the question of her suffering a lingering concern. And without qualifications, we were all suffering as she suffered through her final hours.

I could nevertheless take a step back and become analytical: one of the coping mechanisms humans sometimes deploy to find understanding, if not acceptance, of experiences that can never be fully understood. So, I thought: suffering is fundamental to the human condition. Suffering creates a vivid contrast illuminating joy, happiness, and satisfaction. It is a harsh lesson on the other side of sublime. We all must suffer, whether we choose to or not. There must be value in that which is given in our lives, even though we hope and try to live joyfully and enjoy our brief time on earth.

We have suffered; we are suffering; we will suffer.

This realization reminded me of a book I had read in college entitled *Siddhartha*, a 1922 novel by Hermann Hesse. Through this story, I learned about Gautama, Prince of Kapilvastu, who lived from 566 to 480 B.C. As the son of an Indian warrior-king, he defined his adolescent years with extravagance, self-serving pleasures, and privileges granted only to members of his elevated social caste in India. But a royal life surrounded by luxuries became unfulfilling, and so he wandered into the wider world searching for understanding and then enlightenment. After wrenching encounters with old age, illness, and death, he came to an understanding that suffering constituted the nature and endpoint of all existence. Renouncing his formerly privileged life, he became a monk, depriving himself of all the material wealth and privileges that had dominated his youth. His self-depriving search ended with a long meditative session below a tree wherein he came to the realization of four *Noble Truths* about human existence: suffering exists; suffering has a cause; suffering has an end; and there is a path that can free humans from suffering. Only aging, sickness and death are definite and inescapable. Following this humble monk's epiphany of epochal proportions, Siddhartha became known as the "Enlightened One" or Buddha.

Suffering begets maturation for some of us; we grow wiser as we suffer. Some of us become more resilient as suffering cycles back into our lives. Some of us will do anything to cover up suffering, whether with psychoactive drugs, unbridled consumerism, or rash decisions that end marriages or careers. Some of us commit suicide when suffering can no longer be tolerated. When suffering comes, suffering is in charge. Suffering cannot lose; we can merely arrive at compromises through learning, adaptation, accommodation, and acceptance.

So, is there value in suffering? I recall the misty days following the deaths of our parents so closely contiguous in July 2000. It was as if they had decided to leave together and perhaps distill survivor grief into one concentrated span of time rather than to die months or years apart. Dad had once inspired my brother-in-law, Joel, with a memorable declaration of love for his beloved: "I want to die first so I won't miss her."

Some might suggest that my conscientious parents gave their surviving family members a final gift. We certainly appreciated the unexpected convenience of planning one memorial service for them rather than two separate events located in their hometown hundreds and thousands of miles from our homes. My wife, Becky, wholeheartedly believes that her mother-in-law felt safe to die as soon as Dad left us, and Becky insists his spiritual presence filled their shared nursing home room as my mother began to take her final breaths less than twenty-four hours after Dad.

There is hope in the resurrection, whether it is the story of Jesus Christ or an intuitive feeling that a father or mother have remained intact in a spirit world that we living humans can speculate upon but cannot fully grasp. I accepted Becky's perspective although I felt no sensation of Dad's spiritual presence as Mom died. At the time of a very dramatic twenty-four-hour period in my family's journey, I did not see and could not understand the value in suffering. Their final months seemed more like harsh punishment without mitigating compensation.

I existed in a thick, murky fog for many weeks, slogging through days of routine and work, numb and sad and disillusioned and distracted. That became a dark time when life required me to look squarely at suffering and attempt to glean a modicum of psychological benefits or advantages, to discover an upside of such a significant double loss. The dense fog did not begin to lift until three months later when Becky and I undertook an impetuous journey to a strange and alluring place called Amsterdam, Holland.

I did not merely need a vacation, which, arguably I did. Amsterdam called to me, something akin to a mythic, spiritual calling as described by Joseph Campbell: *a call to adventure.* "This fateful region of both treasure and danger," wrote Campbell, "may be variously represented: as a distant land, a forest, a kingdom, underground, beneath the waves, or above the sky, a secret island, lofty mountaintop, or profound dream state; but it is always a place of strangely fluid and polymorphous beings, unimaginable torments, superhuman deeds, and impossible delight."[11] We were hoping for *impossible delights* rather than *unimaginable torments.*

As I had wanted, we were spellbound with the ancient Dutch city, the canals, exceptionally friendly natives, and an all-pervading creative vibe. From Rembrandt's original painting studio to a modern

---

11 Campbell, Joseph, *The Hero with a Thousand Faces*, Princeton: Princeton University Press, 1990

museum showcasing Vincent van Gogh, we traveled in the footsteps of the Masters. We soaked up the ambiance of the architecture and a captivating blend of modern technology meeting Old World craft. We walked many miles every day and feasted on cuisine from ethnic traditions spanning the globe. We visited a few "coffeeshops," those unique Dutch establishments where cannabis is as common and accepted as a glass of wine or a café latte.

All this stimulation and, yes, escapism, ignited my creativity, which I expressed through photography. I took hundreds of still photos with most images being candid portraits of the Dutch people being themselves, from ubiquitous mothers on bicycles transporting their toddlers, to innovative street buskers and mimes. I found odd juxtapositions of compositional elements, creating more than merely standard travel images; I captured visual stories of a European setting very different from our home city of Denver, Colorado.

My suffering over the loss of my parents opened windows in my mind where I saw things differently. I discovered a way of living that I could not have fully grasped without added gravity of inconsolable loss. I found modernity in a city centuries old. I allowed my senses to take in all that life can offer if we are alert, present, and open to new experiences. And gently, numbing grief transformed into new possibilities: a satellite's perspective of how my life might proceed forward productively, someday feeling more inspired to create and contribute and move forward, chastened by the past but not stymied forever.

We came home from Amsterdam, and I produced a photographic exhibition. I worked for several months to transform 35-mm film transparencies into giant, digitally printed posters. I immersed myself into stimulating details of image perfection through Adobe Photoshop. In the background of my feverish work, I thought about Mom and Dad and what their lives had meant to me: Dad being my moral compass, inspiring determination and a modicum of righteous indignation, and Mom being the wellspring of my unquenchable urge to be creative, whether with words or images or a combination of both.

So, in April 2001, nine months after our parents had passed away, I hosted a photographic exhibition at Stella's, a popular gourmet coffee shop in the Washington Park area of Denver, where my framed Amsterdam photographs remained on display for several weeks. More than fifty friends and family members attended my reception and art show, and I received exactly the compensation I had been seeking: sharing my visual perspective about the joys of living and not suffering.

I am now convinced that without psychic suffering I would not have traveled to Amsterdam when we did; nor would I have seen what I saw: transitory moments when visual elements aligned under optimum lighting conditions; nor would I have been as diligent to capture the images on film; nor would I have been motivated to work hard to achieve some mastery of Photoshop so my photographic images could be enhanced and perfected for digital printing; nor would I have invested time and resources to transform my enhanced images into large format, framed digital prints; nor would I have taken creative risks involved in sharing my work with friends and business associates in a public setting.

Suffering slices deep into the psyche; its dominance can be absolute for a period. When suffering, it is tough to see rainbows and give a damn. Suffering lingers and changes one's outlook. Suffering causes regrets. Suffering inspires. Suffering flips non-being into being.

Actor and screenwriter Sylvester Stallone, who became famous for his breakthrough movie, *Rocky*, the story of a struggling prizefighter, understands regret even from his lofty perch as an A-list Hollywood celebrity: "I have tons of regrets, but I think that's one of the reasons that push people to create things. Out of their angst, their regret, comes the best from artists, painters, and writers."[12]

Suffering made me want to capture a sliver of what is useful and attainable in this life. Suffering caused me to understand better what I had learned from my parents, teachings that I had not fully appreciated or comprehended when they were living. Suffering eventually motivated

---

12 Stallone, Silvester, as quoted by Brainyquotes.com: http://www.brainyquote.com/quotes/quotes/s/sylvesters460525.html

me to re-engage with life and find unexpected ways to bring some permanence to our transitory existence through photos and posters that may survive me. Even though these digitally enhance photographs will never rise to the stature of fine art, nor will they be prized and acquired by others, they will remain after I have gone as a testament to the product of my suffering. I saw what others had not; I felt resurrection of my spirit through creating; I captured fleeting moments in time; I transformed the foreign, figuratively and literally, into the familiar; and I solidified these experiences as digital color posters.

Dr. Harry "Rick" Moody along with co-author David Carroll have extensively explored how our many spiritual passages, including personal losses, can transform us, often with a positive outcome. From one of his university students who had been suffering from a deep depression, Dr. Moody came upon an important insight: *"Your adversary is your helper."*

When we undergo a harsh setback, a crisis, a severe loss, even a prolonged period of sadness or depression, the psychological check valves that keep certain emotions locked inside us are sprung, and powerful new feelings come flooding out.

In the flurry that follows, we find ourselves caught up in the confusion and distress. We endure these bouts of anguish as best we can and hope for the best. There's not always a great deal we can do for ourselves while they're taking place.

But afterward, when the smoke clears and the trauma is past, we discover that certain rock-hard insights have crystallized from those encounters. We find that age-old psychic debris is purged from us now and that we are different and better people for having passed through the needle's eye. Certain notions begin to make sense for the first time, such as the Jewish saying: 'God is closest to those with broken hearts'; or the quote from the Midrash: 'Not to know suffering means not to be human.'

Something that once held us back, that obscured our vision, has been removed; and the suffering is what removed it.[13]

Helen Keller, born with the ability to see and hear, contracted either scarlet fever or meningitis as an infant at nineteen months. The illness ravaged her sensory organs until she became sightless and deaf. Keller was the first blind and deaf person to earn a Bachelor of Arts degree. She then wrote and published twelve books as well as lectured worldwide. She understood suffering from a perspective that would be terrifying to most. She wrote, "Character cannot be developed in ease and quiet. Only through experience of trial and suffering can the soul be strengthened, ambition inspired, and success achieved."[14] And, indeed Keller's indefatigable persistence to learn the language and pursue higher education stands as a hallmark of suffering transformed into self-evolving significance.

Suffering can precipitate creativity, liberating the creator through inspiration and then many available channels of human communication, and therefore *there is value in suffering.*

13 Moody, Harry R., and Carroll, David, *The Five Stages of the Soul: Charting the Spiritual Passages that Shape Our Lives*, Anchor Books, August 1998, page 95 - 96
14 Keller, Helen, as quoted on Values.com: https://goo.gl/mrvwsV

FURTHER QUESTIONS ABOUT
SUFFERING TO CONSIDER

What event or situation has precipitated the greatest suffering during your life?

Do you believe you came to terms with the moments of your greatest suffering? How so?

Did you feel supported in your suffering, a strong shoulder from a loved one, or a religious faith practice?

Assuming we never fully come to terms with suffering, can you find support today?

What forms of creativity can you enthusiastically pursue today that could lend meaning and tangible expression to your suffering?

CAN SOMEONE'S COURAGE TO FACE SUFFERING STRENGTHEN US?

THE BOY LAY pensively inside an oxygen tent, struggling to breathe the cold, aseptic air; nurses and doctors gathered curiously around their little patient. The child became frightened by this sea of white coats, not knowing if their appearance might precede some other invasive treatment for his inability to inhale.

The child had almost died two days earlier from asthmatic broncho-constriction. After an ambulance rushed him to a hospital emergency room and then stabilized his gasping, labored breathing, his heart raced from fear of these doctors plus the speedy effects of epinephrine surging through his bloodstream.

Ten years later, the child had "outgrown" his acute asthma attacks and was becoming a rebellious teenager. Since this was the mid-1960s, around 50 percent of adult men in the United States smoked cigarettes, the 20th-century symbol of iconoclastic culture, the rise of Marlboro Man.

Hollywood icons such as Sammy Davis Jr., Yul Brynner, George Peppard, and Steve McQueen popularized the cool habit—and then died because of it. A monolithic tobacco industry employed marketing trickery to make the dangerous addiction appear benign if not down-right healthful. Smoking had become the cultural norm celebrated in marketing and movies.

The teenager became hooked on nicotine before the United States Surgeon General announced in 1965 that cigarette smoking could be a

cause of lung cancer and other serious diseases. By the time this teenager became a college graduate student in psychology, he had smoked as
many as two packs of cigarettes per day, and lung abuse was beginning
to take a toll on his health.

The person I'm describing is me. An asthmatic in childhood and ad-
dicted to cigarettes in my youth, I owe my health today to a man and a
philosophy of living that he personified. And to me, this man's life also
represents how suffering can be faced and managed and inspired by the
courage of others. The day we first met coincidentally became one of my
life's most significant watershed moments.

At the beginning of my second year of graduate school at the
University of Kansas, several students and I visited a popular professor at her home. During our conversation, her boyfriend stopped by,
a man of imposing stature, at that time weighing around 215 pounds
of solid muscle. At six-foot-four-inches and with a chiseled jaw, Mark
Crooks initially appeared to be a stereotypical jock, albeit one who
could have also posed as a male fashion model. I learned that he was
a Ph.D. candidate seeking double degrees in sports psychology and
exercise physiology.

Mark's extraordinary fitness and his friendly nature caused me to
confess to him that I was then having growing concerns about my health.
By the early 1970s, the connections between smoking and cancer had
gained wider acceptance despite extraordinary denials by tobacco com-
panies coupled with intimidating lawsuits. I knew my long-term health
was on the line. Mark invited me to go jogging with him the following
Saturday, and though hesitant I accepted.

We ran in a city park in Lawrence, and at first, I kept pace, being
young and lean. But as the miles stretched out, Mark's graceful stride
left me in the background. I recall seeing him running effortlessly
ahead in the distance. Because I wanted health more than anything after a childhood punctuated by illnesses, I quit smoking four days later,
on September 14, 1973. Mark never scolded or lectured me about smoking but caused me to seek health because of his example.

In time the details of his story unfolded to me as he cautiously brought me into private areas of his life. I recall one beautiful spring day many years later when we ran together once again in a forest near his home in Kansas City. Mark's life seemed to distill into those rare moments of fitness freedom.

He loped ahead, still a towering athlete but with one remaining lung. The cancer had destroyed his other lung two years earlier, although he had never smoked cigarettes and had been a running pioneer since the 1970s. After our fateful first meeting at the University of Kansas, he had become my benchmark for physical fitness—my inspirational deliverer from seven years of juvenile nicotine addiction—so I always took advantage of our rare opportunities to go jogging together.

Dappled sunlight spilled upon the forested trail where we ran, and I felt elation seeing Dr. Mark Crooks pulling ahead, effortlessly. Though disabled with a single lung, he still could trounce me on the trail. As his wide shoulders and a dark mane of wavy hair shape-shifted into elm tree shadows ahead, I reflected upon self-empowered living that he embodied.

He was a proud man who had learned too much about cancer, pain, and rehabilitation. When we jogged that spring day, he had already survived cancer for fifty-five years, battling nerve, thyroid, and lung cancers. He would face two more metastatic bouts—prostate and liver—before it would be over.

Cancer imposed egregious injustices upon an athlete and former Marine, who had earned a doctoral degree in exercise physiology and had dedicated many years to inspiring and teaching stricken men how to recover from heart attacks. Mark's first mitochondrial mutation had followed a head-and-neck X-ray in infancy: an untested therapy unwisely deployed by a physician to fight an antibiotic resistant sinus infection. Then a sarcoma appeared on his neck at age eight.

But I knew his mind well after three decades of friendship. He wasn't thinking about the injustice of metastatic disease. He was thinking about a beautiful day—fresh air, sweet scents of budding trees, and his daily mastery over inertia. He wasn't trying to intimidate me with superior conditioning either. Mark just ran far and away in the manner he chose to spend part of each day. His only unbeatable competitor was the nemesis lurking within since childhood. Early immersion in mortality propelled his life course and had given him the uncommon determination to fight evil with science, experimentation, and risk-taking.

Most lives cannot be summed up by a single incident; rather, most human stories are collections of actions and reactions, an amalgam becoming a narrative, of plots and subplots spanning decades. This narrative was also true for Mark's story, but in one oddly defining moment, he leaped from the apex of a bridge crossing a dangerous river, plunging ten stories and landing in nine feet of coffee-colored water.

For weeks, he had honed his physique with free weights and running, living a Spartan existence and practicing mid-air orientation through trial jumps from limestone cliffs in the Missouri Ozarks. From successively higher cliffs, he had jumped into space, landing almost splash-less as if a professional cliff jumper. He then selected the Paseo Bridge in Kansas City, a final jump location from which several tortured men had committed suicide.

As he launched into the void from the lip of that bridge, an eighteen-wheeler blasted by him. Wind draft pushed his torso forward, introducing the possibility that he would land imperfectly and break his back. Then in midair, he mounted an invisible bicycle and pedaled for the finish. His body became vertical within a free-fall reaching sixty-three miles per hour, and he slipped splash-less into choppy, murky currents. Seconds later he exploded through the surface, arms extended in Olympic victory.

Jumping from a bridge into a river did not define Mark, but that single courageous act of fitness and determination illuminated his incandescent spirit while elaborating his message: humans can achieve greater wellness by taking calculated risks.

His risks were bold and brash; the doctor became his experiments. He did not advocate for mere mortals to follow in his jump stream. He saw risk as relative: one man's Arctic Circle trek is another man's casual day hike; one woman's skydiving freefall is another woman's tethered zip-line. Risk lies more in the heart of the actor than in the act itself.

Endorphins are a gift for taking risks: opiate pretenders that can reduce pain and create well-being, and, according to some authorities, become the biochemicals of longevity. Those same neurotransmitters had also molded an image of contentment that I witnessed in a super-athletic, one-lung man leaving me to follow his footprints in the damp loam of a Kansas running trail.

I could also see Mark in the flow, and to him, that word meant more than *going with the flow*. Flow means unwavering immersion in activity—the ultimate way to harness emotions in service of high-performance, a loss of reflective self-consciousness. The pinnacle of the flow experience includes feelings of spontaneous joy and rapture. Often achieved through planned risks, flow is one critical wellness strategy to combat stress hormones that always surface with loss. Taoism has for millennia recognized this mindset as "action of inaction" or "doing without doing." A confident man with many reasons to doubt his prowess had conquered uncertainty, depression, and anxiety as he achieved flow transcendence—capturing states of being that had also empowered Michelangelo as the Master painted the Vatican's Sistine Chapel.

Whether swimming 375 miles nonstop in the frigid Missouri River from Kansas City to St. Louis for five grueling days or scaling the exterior of the tallest skyscraper in the Midwest (with no prior technical climbing experience), Mark commanded intense focus with each selected feat. He pushed himself forward with wisdom succinctly articulated by Friedrich Nietzsche, the 19th-century existentialist: "That which does not kill us makes us stronger." That which did not kill Mark made him stronger, and he gained strength with leaps, dives, and near-misses.

Following our final run together, Mark shared his thoughts about aging, disease and decline, an unholy triumvirate that had visited him much too young when compared with most of his peers. "I still have a warrior mentality," he said. "I'm a fighter. My whole life has been about overcoming things. Adopting fitness as a way of life and part of your daily regimen will keep you more mentally stable.

"I still feel that the best of my life is yet to come. I have certain optimism because I don't realize the limitations that most sixty-three-year-old men have."

His hourglass emptied two years later within the solitude of the Kansas City Hospice. Even then he pushed an intravenous cart around the corridors for glorious minutes of independent movement. Though death was at his doorstep, he still defied mortal inevitability, a diminished man but a noble spirit unwilling to submit until left no further options. Maggie Callanan, a wise and tenured hospice nurse and coauthor of *Final Gifts*, acknowledges the purpose and possibilities of this terminal patient's elaborated final months, weeks, and days: "Instead of a last-gasp sprint, death can be a marathon."[15]

Mark Crooks, Ph.D., died on July 8, 2010. He finished life on his terms. He prevailed for decades over disease, depression, and disinterest. He found satisfying self-expression through running shoes and countless T-shirts drenched with sweat. And he defied aging, not to deny the inevitable but to thwart its pace, a warrior to the end.

Mark showed me another way to negotiate suffering. He personified one of the "beautiful people" described by hospice pioneer, Dr. Elisabeth Kubler-Ross: "The most beautiful people we have known are those who have known defeat, known suffering, known struggle, known loss, and have found their way out of those depths. These persons have an appreciation, a sensitivity, and an understanding of life that fills them with

---

15 Callanan, Maggie, *Final Gifts: Understanding the Special Awareness, Needs, and Communications of the Dying*, Simon & Shuster, February 14, 2012,

compassion, gentleness, and a deep loving concern. Beautiful people do not just happen."[16]

He was an intellectual who invested time and scholarship in understanding the recurring cancers that haunted him throughout his adult life. He could speak to medical professionals in their language, citing the most recent clinical research about the treatment of his diseases. He often turned inward through meditation and self-reflection to manage fear and overcome inevitable uncertainties that come with competing and often ambiguous medical choices. He embraced wellness principles and alternative therapeutic modalities to supplement care he received from traditional western medicine. And, he was spiritual in ways I did not expect from a man so grounded in the here and now, so vigorous and athletic, so macho, such a pioneer in the life-affirming field of wellness.

I recall another time when I visited Mark during one of my speaking engagements in the Kansas City area. We had just finished a healthy meal: large, sumptuous salads composed of ingredients circumnavigating a bountiful garden, vegetables showcasing the colors of a rainbow. Healthy organic stuff. He asked me quite plainly if I believed in God. I answered with an equal directness that I did believe although I was not involved in a denominational church tradition at that period of my life, such as the Protestantism that had baptized me in the Christian faith and characterized my childhood. I asked the same question of him: "How about you? Do you believe in God, Mark?"

Mark opened his heart. He said he felt the presence of the Holy Spirit almost every waking moment of his life. He often had conversations with God as he jogged, which almost always involved running along trails bisecting forests near his home. He knew God was nearby; he knew there would be eternal life after life, and he felt God's grace even as he had to face much uncertainty and so many medical procedures as a perpetual cancer victim.

---

16 Kubler-Ross, Elisabeth, as quoted on Values.com: https://goo.gl/zmAZ0Y

I recall profoundly feeling moved by Mark's declaration of his deepest spiritual feelings. I did not expect to hear statements of faith from a long-term friend who had never spoken to me before about God's goodness and his earnest optimism about a conclusion of his suffering after the end of his life. I had always thought of him as tough, virile, a man's man, grounded in the daily challenges of providing for his family and being a thought leader in the field of wellness. I felt honored and humbled that he trusted me enough to reveal these most private aspects of his spiritual life. With his declaration of faith, communicated with the certitude of a scientist, I too felt a presence of the Holy Spirit hovering over the dining room table as Mark helped me understand what he saw in his heart.

During the many years of our relationship, I felt great empathy for my friend, as one form of cancer after another emerged to challenge him. I felt sympathy for his suffering that surely clawed at his daily routines, always active and busy, but he rarely verbalized complaints while courageously challenging his archenemy. He met pain and physical decline with 600-calorie workouts; he discarded anxieties somewhere along innumerable running trails; he faced death by running through life at full stride.

I also felt confidence that Mark knew what to do to participate actively in his treatments and rehabilitation, and that he would prevail. I didn't give up believing this until he could prevail no more—and then I knew in my heart that God would welcome Mark to eternal life and His grace. I believe Mark is sometimes with me now as I work out, inspiring me to run a little faster or lift more weight. Mark whispers to me when no one else can hear, "Make the world your gymnasium, Brent."

Mark's courage will always be a benchmark in my life as inevitable old-age illnesses and physical decline become nuisances during my final years and months. Like Mark, I plan to push IV carts defiantly in front of me and keep moving until I cannot move anymore. I plan to keep my running shoes tied until the end.

QUESTIONS ABOUT LEARNING FROM THE SUFFERING OF OTHERS

Who has inspired you to face suffering with greater courage and determination and why did this person influence you?

When pain invades your life, how would you ideally like to handle the discomforts, anxieties, and uncertainties?

Have you known someone like Mark Crooks who took on suffering as if a test of will and a challenge to defeat?

What have you learned about suffering from others that you could share with your children and grandchildren to instruct them about resilience and courage in the face of sickness and disease?

How would you now like to prepare yourself better to face suffering that could inspire and instruct others you love?

HAVE YOU EVER EXPERIENCED DESPERATION?

I RECALL A significant day when I met a ten-year-old child who eventually inspired an entire community with her optimism, sense of humor, and extreme confidence before news media. Meeting her began merely as part of my job responsibilities as an advertising account supervisor for McDonald's of Southern Colorado. I was invested in the success of a fundraising program more than in the success of our young charge who would represent our fundraiser. But that changed quickly.

Perhaps no high-profile company has done a better job than McDonald's Corporation has at executing public relations strategies. The corporation's signature Ronald McDonald House (RMH) remains unrivaled in concept and execution.

Throughout the country in major metropolitan areas and many foreign countries, McDonald's has provided leadership and resources to help build, remodel and fund operations for large homes located near major hospitals. *The House that Love Built* provides shelter and sanctuary for parents with children who are receiving long-term medical treatment for diseases such as cancer and diabetes. The RMH provides a structured homelike setting, staffed by professional volunteers, where parents can stay indefinitely while a child receives chemotherapy, dialysis, or other long-term medical treatments. If parents are financially unable to pay a small daily rental fee, always substantially lower than neighboring motels and hotels, then they can stay at the RMH for free if necessary without being charged.

McDonald's reports overseeing 322 Ronald McDonald Houses in fifty-seven countries. Since 1974, RMH programs have helped tens of millions of families with the assistance of thousands of volunteers, donating millions of hours. More than 7,200 bedrooms worldwide provide a respite for families every night.

McDonald's Corporation and local franchisees have made this fundraising challenge a keystone of their annual cause-related marketing programs. Customers embrace the worthwhile spirit of this cause by dropping pocket change in counter displays throughout the year, and now and then by participating in more focused fundraising efforts to support major renovations and building additions.

Early in my marketing career, I served as an account supervisor for an advertising agency that managed promotions and public relations for sixteen McDonald's stores in Southern Colorado, including Colorado Springs. Children from our marketing territory requiring prolonged medical treatment often traveled to Children's Hospital in Denver. Denver franchisees invited store owners in my area to help raise money to support an ambitious renovation of the Denver house. The Denver RMH was short of space because of increasing demand, so the company decided to expand usable space by renovating parts of a third floor and attic. My agency team developed a unique fundraising idea.

An entrepreneurial company approached us, coincidentally, proposing to convert some of the classic 3-D movies from the 1950's and re-broadcast them on television. This novel broadcast technology could preserve the 3-D effects, thus bringing the visual excitement of 3-D into viewers' homes for the first time. However, to watch a 3-D movie on television, home viewers would still need 3-D glasses, those weird sunglasses with one side of the frame covered by red plastic and the other side covered by blue plastic.

We embraced the nostalgia and fun of this idea and agreed to sell 3-D glasses through all sixteen McDonald's restaurants in our marketing territory. Our community's NBC affiliate decided to broadcast the movie for a nominal advertising charge, which was well within the existing advertising budget. All proceeds from the sale of 3-D glasses would be donated to the Denver Ronald McDonald House.

Our agency creative team proceeded to design freestanding promotional displays for each store. We also created television and radio commercials for mass marketing.

The second facet of this program involved building public awareness of the purpose and value of the Denver RMH for families living in Southern Colorado. To make this appeal vivid and emotional, we enlisted help from a single mother whose youngest daughter had been receiving cancer treatments at Children's Hospital.

Ten-year-old Laurel was the ideal child for our publicity campaign. She was energetic, gregarious, optimistic, and fun-loving. We created a television news documentary about Laurel and her family, and we portrayed many difficulties this family had encountered in managing cancer treatments far away from home and friends.

The RMH had served this family well by providing sanctuary and stability during Laurel's chemotherapy treatments. Katherine, Laurel's mother, was an actual beneficiary because Katherine could not hold down a full-time job with Laurel being sick so often and periodically needing aggressive treatments over a protracted period. Katherine did not have adequate financial resources, and she discovered home and heart and hearth at the Ronald McDonald House. She also made critical connections with other parents who were experiencing similar ordeals.

The 3-D movie premiere received substantial publicity and promotion from our media partners, including the NBC affiliate; KILO, a ratings-leading rock 'n' roll radio station; and *The Gazette*, the daily community newspaper. During the final day before the movie premiere, lines of customers encircled the restaurants as people clamored to purchase their special 3-D glasses. All major media covered the promotion as news stories, and we received hundreds of newspaper column inches and nearly an hour of cumulative broadcast television news coverage. Our NBC partner even ran a five-part news series every night for five nights preceding the premiere.

Tiny Laurel became a local celebrity, with her story becoming a focus of an entire community. She accepted a proclamation from the mayor. She appeared at stores with her hero, Ronald McDonald. She became a vivacious subject of dozens of news interviews. She embodied both the desperations of childhood cancer and the hope restored by a unique home far away from home.

McDonald's sold tens of thousands of the 3-D glasses and eventually donated generously to the Denver Ronald McDonald House. The promotion received publicity valued at hundreds of thousands of dollars. Parents answered our fundraising call by donating time, resources, and support to the worthwhile cause. Every customer became a philanthropist by just purchasing a pair of 3-D glasses. Many added to cash donations at counter displays. Moreover, all sixteen stores in our marketing territory experienced substantial sales increases during the promotion because of incremental store traffic.

Sadly, I said goodbye to Laurel two years later at her memorial service, and my memories today remain ragged, a quality of despair that never entirely diminishes. The final chapter of her story unfolds like this:

AFRAID TO JUMP

Thin lips clenched in protest over eyes sewn shut, and her long, black lashes appeared matted—perhaps wet with tears? The scar on her neck was about one-half inch long and dark. Her miniature hands rested palms down on her chest and her fingernails, painted an antique rose, were too long for a child's. Her hands looked bony, though, and I could see dark veins trailing from her knuckles and up her arms. Short sable hair—almost boyish looking—had not grown back. Nose perfectly curved, a face round and full, she was neither gaunt nor sunken as most ravaged by cancer.

She rested inside a hefty, oak-stained coffin. A viewing room had been crammed with floral arrangements: white roses, spring daisies, red roses, daffodils, and one small vase full of wispy Baby's Breath. I had contributed a thin-necked vase clutching two Calla Lilies.

Laurel's favorite subject had been math, but she also loved to read fairy tales with their promises of impossibilities. She had gone to school until a week before she died. She had been ready, although she had not been entirely accepting. Who could be? She had gone to church every Sunday with Katherine and Terra, but we had never talked about God or dying. She had believed in the myth of resurrection and had cried when we watched the Steven Spielberg movie *E.T. the Extra-Terrestrial*. I wouldn't argue that she had been brave about death, but she had never seemed afraid, either.

"She gripped the guardrails as if she might tumble down Seven Falls. She stared far into the canyon," Jeff said. "You should have seen her sudden fear. Alarming."

Huddled in a corner, Terra stared at Jeff and me. She shivered and wiped her swollen nose. I felt like hugging Laurel's sister, but I had never touched her before, and I wasn't sure if I could. Though Terra was just thirteen, she appeared then to be a grown woman.

"She begged us to drive her to Seven Falls," Jeff persisted. "She looked so weak when I picked them up. But she wanted to go more than anything, so Katherine and I said okay."

She wore a white dress with tiny blue flowers. Short, billowy sleeves made her lank arms appear thinner. Her skin was not chalk-white as I had expected; you could still see that Laurel had been dark complexioned. But blue highlights cast her cheeks almost ceramic.

Laurel would have loved nursing. She had spent her final three years lying in hospital beds and accepting painful, nauseating therapies. Oncologists had found the first tumor in a kidney. They excised the kidney, and her prognosis looked good for a year. The cancer metastasized, and they found several small tumors in her neck. They removed those tumors also. That's when she got the dark scar—about half-an-inch long—on her neck. Then they found another tumor in her right lung, perilously near her aorta, inoperable.

Jeff glanced at the coffin. "I don't know why she wanted to go to the Falls. She slept while we drove up. But she walked by herself from the car to the observation deck. She looked over the rails and suddenly recoiled, scared to death..."

Katherine, eyes red and puffy, walked into the room and spotted Jeff. She said, "You're the best Ronald McDonald in the world."

Jeff blushed and hugged her. Out of costume, he looked nothing like McDonald's famous trademark. He had a balding head; a fringe of fuzzy brown hair dangled down his neck; steel blue eyes and wide shoulders made him appear as if an aging football player, not a clown.

"Laurel lives on within us," Jeff said sheepishly.

Katherine broke into tears and rushed across the room. She hugged her only living daughter and buried her head in Terra's blouse.

Jeff wandered with me closer to the coffin. He laid his gigantic right hand on her head as if feeling for fever—or pulse. "I wasn't sure why the canyon scared her so much. It just occurred to me. It wasn't fear of heights. She was afraid to die."

Lying down, a doll's eyes close. When you sit the doll up, eyes open again. Down, closed. Up, open. It seemed morbid, but I wanted to sit Laurel up. I wanted to see her big brown eyes once again.

Then Jeff said, "Katherine told me we shouldn't drive by your office, even though Laurel asked me to stop by the hotel. You're always so busy at work. So, we drove back to their house. She just stared out the car window, saying nothing."

The Calla Lilies smelled too sweet, and I cursed myself for choosing them. Her larynx was prominent, and the long half-inch scar had healed, and it was evident. Her head rested on a single satin pillow, barely denting shimmering fabric.

Jeff sighed and shook his head. "After we got back to their home, she limped to her room, laid down, fell asleep, and died. She didn't hurt too much. But you know Laurel, she never complained."

Her fingernails had grown too long for a ten-year-old girl, though they had been neatly manicured and polished. Perhaps they suggested zesty years ahead. Her imaginary life had become a flower garden of possibilities. So, perhaps, a nurse.

Good grades had been easy for a girl with priorities. She grew up tall and thin, a delicate but determined face. She did well in nursing school because she loved to care for others, and she studied hard because she understood the alternatives: childhood poverty can be a great motivator. And though she resolutely propelled through nursing school, she found time to fall in love with a medical student in residence at the same hospital, a man who, like Laurel, cherished nobler motives for seeking medicine as a career. He loved her exuberance, her robust tan skin, those long, feminine fingers, perfectly manicured nails, and puppy-brown eyes. One evening, perhaps, they exchanged eternal vows.

Her eyes would not open if I sat her up because they had been sewn shut.

"You okay?" Jeff said.

When E.T., the Lilliputian extraterrestrial movie character, lay on an operating room table, he was bloated, lifeless, and his skin had become ghastly chartreuse. Laurel sat stiffly beside me with huge tears running down her cheeks. I felt stupid and mortified for bringing a cancer-stricken girl to a movie so brazenly conveying death. I grabbed her cupped hands, then frozen into a tight, unyielding clench. Then the miracle. A life force pulsed through E.T., and he opened his eyes. His heart light glowed again, and brightly he said, "E.T. phone home. Phone home, phone home!" Joy spread across Laurel's face. She grabbed my hand and squeezed. Light from the movie screen made her face glow, and tear trails, which had traced down her cheeks, glistened.

Jeff leaned over the coffin again and seemed to pray. I had never thought of him as a reverent man; for goodness sake, he made his income as a silly corporate clown.

"Listen," Jeff said. "I know you feel terrible because you didn't visit the hospital last month. Laurel knew you are very busy with your job."

He hung his head and stared at the floor between us. His eyes darted from Calla Lilies back to her face. "So, what do you say we push out of here?"

A few seconds later he said, "You understand?"

Then he said, "A few more minutes, and we ought to let the family alone."

The plump pillow caused her head to push forward at a disquieting angle. You couldn't sleep with your head propped up so high—especially for eternity. Eyes sewn shut, mouth wired tight, she had only ten years to play, laugh, learn—to hope for the miracle that had been E.T.'s.

A few weeks after the movie, I stopped by Laurel's house on a sunny afternoon. She rushed out of her stucco home to greet me as always. I reached inside my car behind the passenger seat and grabbed a fuzzy, stuffed E.T. doll. Like that moment when the extraterrestrial had come back to life, her face became resplendent joy.

Jeff patted her sparrow arm, grabbed me gently by the neck and pushed me toward the door. He nodded politely at Katherine and Terra. "You'll be all right," he said to me.

Then he said, "Let's grab a cup of coffee and talk about it."

My legs moved involuntarily toward the door. I waved at Laurel's mother and sister and then jerked my head quickly left to right to search the room. Jeff kept nudging me out of the chamber, but I didn't see E.T.

Then he said, "It's okay. Laurel's at rest now. God has her. Let's talk about it."

She was tiny for her years, much smaller than her friends. She was lifeless and dainty. Eyes sewn shut; mouth wired tight, her lips looked tight and thin. Her polished fingernails were much too long. The half-inch scar on her neck was dark but had healed.

"You've got to talk about it," Jeff said.

Instead of following Jeff's sage advice and talking about it, I have chosen to write about Laurel and her impact on my life and in doing so,

I look again at desperation and how it can shape our lives. We have all experienced distress to some degree. But this question invites us to look beyond the immediate crisis, obstacle or challenge and consider desperation broadly in our lives. Do we live as if desperation is the major theme that informs our perspective, sets our expectations, and triggers our reactions, some of which can be self-limiting and self-defeating?

A young Welsh poet by the name of Dylan Thomas (1914—1963) channeled his desperation and bitterness into a poem as his father lay dying:

> Do not go gentle into that good night
> Old age should burn and rave at close of day;
> Rage, rage against the dying of the light.
> And you, my father, there on the sad height,
> Curse, bless, me now with your fierce tears, I pray.
> Do not go gentle into that good night.
> Rage, rage against the dying of the light.[17]

My encounter with desperation while witnessing the death of a precious child changed me, teaching me that although we will have sad times, we can move on, chastened and changed but resilient and hopeful. Laurel showed me one way to live with hope as well as cancer as she thrived even when tumors grew within her small body. She exhibited how a child can push aside despair and appreciate as many moments as possible, to believe in the power of resurrection, both the human spirit and in a Biblical sense.

In his best-selling novel, *All the Light We Cannot See*, author Anthony Doerr, reminded me of the brevity of desperation in a larger cosmic context: "How long do these intolerable moments last for God? A trillionth of a second? The very life of any creature is a quick-fading spark

---

17 Thomas, Dylan, *The Poems of Dylan Thomas*, Copyright 1952, New Directions

in fathomless darkness. That's God's truth."[18] Brevity is an exact description of desperation also: it will come, it will challenge us, and then it will leave for a time, opening opportunities for renewed faith, optimism, and greater access to fulfillment.

18   Doerr, Anthony, *All the Light We Cannot See: A Novel*, Schribner (2014), 419

QUESTIONS TO ASK WHEN DESPAIR COMES

Do you understand all factors that are contributing to your despair?

If you could change one thing about your situation, what would you change and how could this change soften your raw feelings of hopelessness?

How are others around you being impacted by your despair, and what can you do to help someone else who is connected to the same situation?

What lessons are you learning from your situation that can help you better cope with future life events that will likely trigger despair?

Can there be a resurrection of your spirit in the living world by understanding your situation from a different perspective and finding a path to move forward?

DO YOU BELIEVE IN THE POWER OF FORGIVENESS?

⌐ ⌐

MANY YEARS AGO, I realized that others could malign and reject me. Most of us learn these harsh lessons early, whether the unsavory side of our social education comes in the form of cruel teasing in elementary school or an abrupt and inexplicable rejection by a teenage boyfriend or girlfriend. Being cast away by someone we trust, respect, or love is one of life's harshest reminders that nothing is permanent and, perhaps, others we have learned to depend on can be inherently undependable.

Remember with me for a moment how you first learned to be more guarded with your trust. How old were you? Who became your unexpected antagonist? Who permanently changed you, making you more cautious, suspicious, or guarded?

I recall a friend in high school who had charmed me with his wit, gaiety, and affable personality. People seemed to love Robert wherever we went. He was popular with girls and respected by boys. He was mature for his age, the source of which I did not understand but admired. He gave me glimpses of how I too would develop with more time passing. We became almost inseparable, spending many hours together after school and occasionally on exhilarating double dates.

One time Robert invited me to his home after school. It was a squatty cinder-block house not much larger than 1,200 square feet. Although my parents were middle-class people living in a comfortable but understated middle-class house that my father had supervised in construction, my childhood home was a castle compared to Robert's. His family was economically challenged, and back then I observed those economic disparities but did not care. Affluence or lack thereof had little impact on my appreciation of others. Our friendship was where I found wealth. Robert never apologized for his family's economic situation nor did he seem self-conscious about his parents' relative poverty. That day after school we had visited a nearby city park and recreation center and then ended up at his cinder-block house and his bedroom where we listened to The Beatles and other popular music of that time. I recall his energy, optimism, and ironic take on almost everything. Robert provided me everything I needed in a male friendship at that point in my life.

My father had earlier that day given me a weekly allowance, which I earned through myriad chores around the home; the sum was five dollars, a lot at that time. For some reason, I showed Robert the contents of my wallet when I removed the billfold from my jeans during a period of roughhousing.

Later that evening after I returned home, I discovered an empty wallet, and this was a source of enormous anxiety and loss: an entire week of spending money vanished, and, as importantly, feelings of self-deprecation for losing my allowance. I called Robert to see if he had found a five-dollar bill. He told me that indeed he had found five dollars earlier that night in his front yard, but he was confident that the money did not belong to me. In the vernacular of the time, his discovery was "finders-keepers."

At first I was dumbstruck, disbelieving that Robert expected me to accept that my loss had nothing to do with his good fortune, that a five-dollar bill had magically appeared in his front yard, and it was not the same bill I had shown him earlier that evening. Feelings of betrayal constituted my delayed reaction. I did not believe his story, and I told him so. I did not censor my anger. Even though he stubbornly tried to persuade me that his discovery had nothing to do with my loss, I did not believe him. The obvious connection between my loss and his discovery became too compelling to shove aside.

So, I rejected Robert. I cut him out of my life and never spoke with him again although we continued to pass by each other as we traveled around our high school campus. Whether guilty of theft or not, he did not make any attempts to restore our friendship either, which I interpreted even then as de facto evidence of his dishonesty and guilt. On a few occasions that our paths crossed following high school graduation, I acted as if I didn't even know him, never acknowledging his presence. He did the same.

But I remain haunted by one lingering doubt: What if Robert's version of the missing five-dollar bill had been truthful after all? What if he had found a different bill than I had lost that same night? Further to confuse my righteous indignation, another moral question, requiring greater maturity, lingered: So, what if Robert stole my money? He was from an impoverished family, and he probably spent private time feeling the oppression and humiliation of being underprivileged in a high school setting populated by sons and daughters of many wealthy parents. Perhaps it would have been generous, and much nobler of me, to have merely given Robert my permission to keep the money without further censure or rejection. Maybe we would have both grown more mature when recognizing that the benefits of our friendship trumped a small amount of money. I suspect that the five-dollar bill to Robert was more than he ever received from his parents if he ever had been given an allowance because he worked part-time clerking at a local drug store to earn spending money. Maybe he would have paid me back someday.

I never forgave Robert, so I must now confess that the potential power of forgiveness has eluded me more often than restoring my faith in others. There have been a handful of additional friends and girlfriends like Robert, who have come and gone from my life, former friends and lovers who in my judgment have violated my trust or failed to maintain equanimity in our relationships. And I have cut those newer bad actors from the story of my life as well. And before I go overboard with self-condemnation for being doctrinaire, few of those who I have rejected for my perceptions of bad faith have attempted to restore our relationships.

But, thankfully, a few have returned and forgiven me as I have vindicated them, and those people nourish me today even though we are separated by many miles and impracticalities that distance brings to daily engagement. Some of "the forgiven" are Facebook friends now, where we can be part of each other's lives through periodic updates and posts. I am glad these special people from my earlier life story have been willing to include me in their lives today, even if it's the arms-length channel of a digital social network. But their virtual presence is nourishing, reassuring, and rejuvenating. They have a perspective that is rare: they understand the people we once were when much younger, as well as the people we have become today.

So, I have pushed through some barriers to forgiveness—ego, insecurity, anger, dogmatism, self-righteous indignation, and mistrust—to understand better the life-affirming benefits of simply forgiving others for injustices I have experienced, whether real or imagined. And, importantly, I have learned to forgive myself for having been slow or resistant to forgive.

After writing the sentences above, I jumped online in a moment of curiosity to see if a Google keyword search could help me find Robert if he still exists because it has been fifty-plus years since the fateful night that ended our friendship. I tried several search strings involving his name and last known geographic location.

Robert does not exist anymore, at least in the online realm. I also checked LinkedIn and Facebook just to exhaust any other possibilities that he has a digital footprint capable of leading me to him today. I'm pretty good at online searches, so I can safely conclude there is no path back to this former friend from afar—even if my only purpose would be to satisfy my curiosity and perhaps lurk a bit on his Facebook wall or, by examining his LinkedIn professional profile, learn how his career and life have progressed since we were teens.

Thus, I'm left with two options. I can leave Robert in my mental rejection file where my memory of him has been funneled for five decades. I can forgive him though he'll never know—if he is even alive today—that my thoughts and better intentions have returned to our former friendship. I can forgive him because maybe he never deserved my harsh rejection. I can forgive him because the reason for my indignation is stupid: five dollars is meaningless in the context of a lifetime of earnings. I can forgive him because in doing so I forgive myself for fearing betrayal or being too slow to understand the other person's perspective—for lacking empathy and charity. I can forgive Robert and thus lessen one burden from my life's accumulation of regrets and second-guesses. And I can forgive myself for being judgmental of the behavior of others when I never completely understood the full context.

Forgiveness is a conscious choice to become more liberated and less constrained by the past. This simple act of changing one's mindset can be the wellspring of tolerance, mercy, and compassion.

So, Robert, wherever you are, I forgive you, and I forgive myself for casting you away without honest communication between us, leading to a complete understanding, or at least reasonable sympathy for your life situation. Some inherent part of me once saw you as a splendid person, charming and upbeat. You filled some of the toughest days of my high school journey with excitement, empowerment, and energy. Your maturity gave me additional perspective about what it means to leave adolescence behind and become an adult. Your allure among our female classmates provided me with a few dates I would not otherwise have had. So, thank you for what you gave me when I needed it. I will now endeavor only to honor what was valuable in our friendship.

A lesson I've learned since Robert and I hung out together came to me lyrically through a stirring song written and performed by Don Henley, co-founder of a 1970s country-rock supergroup called the Eagles. In "The Heart of the Matter," Henley points to the crux of forgiveness:

"There are people in your life
Who've come and gone,

They let you down,
You know they've hurt your pride.
You better put it all behind you;
'Cause life goes on.
If you keep carryin' that anger,
It'll eat you up inside baby."[19]

Although the lyrics suggest he is sending a message to a former girlfriend or lover, Henley also had a major split-up with the Eagles and co-founder Glenn Frey in July 1980. Not only did disagreements within the band fracture their friendship and creative partnership, for many years after that the likelihood of a band reunion became as probable as "when hell freezes over." But time passing and irresistible economic opportunities led these two influential musicians toward reconciliation in the early 1990's and a sensible decision to restore one of the most endearing and influential rock music groups of the twentieth century. They recorded a new album appropriately entitled "Hell Freezes Over" and began another ascent to the top of the music charts along with sold-out concerts worldwide.

Glenn Frey also alluded to the power of letting go and forgiving through his inspired song, "It's Your World Now."

"It's your world now
My race is run
I'm moving on
Like the setting sun
No sad goodbyes
No tears allowed
You'll be alright
It's your world now."[20]

---

19 "The Heart of the Matter," words and music by Don Henley, Mike Campbell, and J.D. Souther, copyright 1989
20 "It's Your World Now," performed by The Eagles, words and music by Glenn Frey and Jack Tempchin, copyright 2007

With Glenn Frey's untimely and unexpected death at age 67 in January 2016, the Eagles became part of music history, just as The Beatles concluded forevermore with the assassination of John Lennon in December 1980. But the Eagles ended their "long run" on a high note and intact thanks to the power of forgiveness. Part of the band's legacy *is the power of forgiveness.*

William B. Silverman and Kenneth Cinnamon, also a lifelong friend and college roommate, wrote and published a helpful book entitled *When Mourning Comes: A Book of Comfort for the Grieving.* The authors addressed forgiveness and its importance to healing and unencumbered living:

> As God forgives, so we must forgive, both the dead and ourselves. As God has forgiven us for mortal limitations and fallibilities, so we must forgive. We must rid ourselves of our locked-in guilt, anger, hurt, and resentments. We must bury the hurt, and take a last look at the real or imagined guilt we feel before we enter it in the tomb of yesterday. We need the humility to realize that perfection is reserved for God, the humility that allows us to accept our fallibility as human beings. This will help us to say of our feelings of guilt and self-reproach, "This too shall pass."
>
> We can then love our loved ones who are still alive with an added tenderness because the days of love are short. When mourning comes, we should be reminded that there is a time to hold and a time to let go. Believing that God has made everything beautiful in its time, now is the time when we should *love* and let die. Now is the time when we should *live* and let die.[21]

Forgiveness often requires both parties to forgive. But sometimes we do make bad choices about our friendships and confidants, never

---

21 Silverman, William B. and Cinnamon, Kenneth M., *When Mourning Comes: A Book of Comfort for the Grieving*, Nelson-Hall of Chicago, pg. 44

discovering and accepting all aspects of a friend's behavior and loyalty. Making bad choices is particularly the case for those of us in middle age and older. We accumulate relationship baggage over time, and sometimes it may be smarter to jettison a relationship rather than assume that noble acts of forgiveness will be shared and reciprocated. For this reason and to add to the dialectic of this discussion, I have given the various kinds of friendship some thought and come to the following conclusions about whom to forgive and whom to bid farewell. Sometimes *intentional loss,* a way of forgiving yourself for making a misjudgment earlier in life, can be a necessary prelude to growth and maturation.

AGING AND THREE KINDS OF FRIENDSHIP

An accepted pillar of healthy aging involves fostering nurturing affiliations with others. The late Beatle John Lennon counseled, "Count your age by friends, not years."

One of the ruthless risks of aging is social isolation. Career contacts disappear. Older family members pass away. Nearby friends retire elsewhere. Children relocate to pursue blossoming careers. Some friends die too soon.

A "third age" without rewarding friendships can make us sicker faster and even contribute to an early demise. A recent article in *Nature* reported in the Proceedings of the National Academy of Sciences, which concluded that "limited contact with family, friends and community groups predicts illness and earlier death, regardless of whether it is accompanied by feelings of loneliness."[22]

Feeling lonely may be an existential fact of living that we can survive; being socially isolated, however, may be a death sentence. It follows that one key to healthy aging comes from real companionship.

---

22 Mascarelli, Amanda, "Social isolation shortens lifespan," *Nature: International Weekly Journal of Science*, March 25, 2013, https://goo.gl/iv7kK6

Some friendships gathered over a lifetime, we learn, are not real. Those friends become frustrating and exhausting. They don't have the time or desire to burden themselves with our problems. Some want social activities to be all fun, all the time, and others need friendships to be all about them.

Now that I'm moving through the "third age" of life, I recognize the necessity to abandon unhealthy friendships and nurture those who are committed to the joys and responsibilities that real closeness can bring. I have learned to think more critically about the quality of friendships, not merely quantity.

CONVENIENCE FRIENDSHIPS

Many friendships germinate because of circumstances. Research from the field of social psychology validates that physical proximity is the most significant factor contributing to relationships of substance. The *proximity principle* suggests that we form close relationships with those who are geographically near us. People who frequently encounter each other develop strong bonds.

Thus, we pick up convenient friendships as we travel through life: childhood neighbors, school classmates, people we work with early in our careers, and associates we meet through professional and civic organizations.

And while convenience friendships can be miracles in our lives, knitting together decades of shared experiences, sometimes these relationships survive as old habits growing tattered with time. Friendships based on convenience can fall out of balance, even growth restricting.

I learned about the shortcomings of a convenient friendship early in life. One boy from the neighborhood was a year older, taller, and became the alpha male in our relationship. We spent a lot of time together, inseparable.

Whatever was on his agenda became a priority for me. He found a job delivering newspapers to earn spending money; I scrambled to do the same. He began smoking cigarettes; I took up the habit. He became rebellious toward authority as a teenager; I too became a budding iconoclast.

As we grew older, I eventually realized that the power in the relationship was skewed toward him. He sometimes could be psychologically menacing. He taunted me for being smaller and less athletic. He teased me about my clothes as we became hyper-conscious of rigid adolescent fashions. He sometimes dismissed me when other friends his age came to visit.

I eventually realized that this boyhood relationship, while convenient, did not offer me much fulfillment. I grew weary of his dominant personality and unwillingness to give me credit for having unique value and talents. So, when he moved away to start his career after college, I let him go his way and haven't been in touch for over forty years. He has never reached out to me either, so I guess he also realized that when proximity ended, so did impetus for us to stay in touch.

COSMETIC FRIENDSHIPS

Earlier in my career, I was responsible for managing significant advertising budgets. I was popular with media sales representatives, and one of them charmed me with his wit. He became a fun friend, and we would often meet for cocktails after work. He escorted me to the ski slopes and helped me become a proficient downhill skier, a personal triumph, much appreciated. My fondness for him grew, and he seemed genuine in his positive regard for me.

Eventually, I left the job with oversight of substantial ad budgets that benefited this friend, who worked as a sales representative for a radio station. He soon became scarce and unavailable. And finally an insight came to me: He was not my friend because of positive feelings for me; he *acted* like my friend because I could benefit him financially and status-wise within a cloistered media community.

Most of us have had cosmetic friends like my example. Our job status made them feel more important while providing access to our social networks. We could help them achieve a goal, financial or otherwise. When our status changed, they abandoned the friendship. Gone and forgotten.

INTERDEPENDENT FRIENDSHIPS

Interdependent relationships are the healthiest. Both parties contribute and receive. Both are available to share the benefits of closeness and help shoulder the burdens that appear as we age. They are committed to mutual growth and positive adaptation along the uncharted journey through life.

One of my closest friends, described in an earlier chapter, whom I met during college, was this kind of person. Sometimes our contacts would be infrequent because of geographical distance, but we would periodically reach out to each other and be available for support as needed. I helped him through a divorce as a sympathetic advisor, and he helped me embrace a wellness lifestyle that eluded me when I was a cigarette smoker.

Many years later I helped him manage the injustices of cancer, reminding him of his innate strengths and wisdom. I helped convince him to accept hospice care when it became apparent that further heroic medicine would not extend his life. He showed me how to die with grace.

As I've grown older and wiser, I've become more aware that not all friendships are created equal. Convenience friendships may benefit from shared history, but sometimes these attachments were never appropriate in the first place. We experience loss before we lose the relationship.

Cosmetic friendships are usually fleeting: when our status or value to the other person diminishes, they depart without even saying goodbye.

Interdependent friendships can be one gift of maturity: the few amazing friends we can count on when we become distraught or disillusioned. They are the friends who lift our spirits and in return welcome a sympathetic shoulder during their tough times.

As I reflect upon my friendships through life, I accept that I have not always been above self-centeredness and pretense that can inspire convenient or cosmetic friendships. Maturity compels me to accept and correct my relationship deficiencies so that I can become a better friend. Aging has taught me that less can be more as I aim for interdependent friendships, stable, and sustainable.

Charles Caleb Colton, a popular nineteenth-century English cleric, advised, "Books, like friends, should be few and well chosen."

QUESTIONS TO CONSIDER ABOUT FORGIVENESS

Have you ever been forgiven by someone you love when you felt fully exonerated and fully accepted once again?

Have you ever forgiven someone else, meant it, and received the injured party's forgiveness in return?

Whom do you wish to forgive now? Why? How? When?

Can you find someone who injured you earlier in your life through online social networks? Will you now extend an olive branch and ask for and give forgiveness?

If there is an estranged someone from your past who is no longer living, will you forgive them now?

Can forgiveness liberate you from the psychic pain you carry, as suggested in Don Henley's song, "The Heart of the Matter"?

FURTHER QUESTIONS TO CONSIDER ABOUT FORGIVENESS

Can we forgive forever?

Does your lifetime of relationships provide examples of genuine and enduring forgiveness?

Whom have you never forgiven? Are there possible circumstances under which your forgiveness could be forthcoming?

If you could be forgiven by someone who believes you injured them, how would the act of forgiveness come about that would be most satisfying and complete for you. A face-to-face meeting? An instant message? A telephone call? A Facebook post?

What person are you willing to forgive who never got to know you, a person who never seemingly gave you a chance to become a real person in their minds?

WHAT WAS YOUR FIRST EVER EXPERIENCE OF LOSS?

GRANDPARENTS USUALLY ARE the first to leave us. After years of struggle with heart disease, my father's father, William Thomas Green, began the procession and eventual departure of four grandparents. Since I was just fourteen then, I barely remember his funeral, although I retain a few mental glimpses of a large turnout from members of a small western Kansas farming community where he had lived and sold real estate. I recall seeing my father and uncle crying for the first time. Grandpa Green had been a respected man about town and somewhat prosperous, although the Great Depression had wreaked havoc on his accumulating real estate portfolio. Many showed up to pay their respects that day. I absorbed the surrounding sadness and had my first memorable encounter with the permanence of death as well as a more nuanced understanding that someday I would also die. To a fourteen-year-old mostly sheltered from intimate encounters with death, this was difficult. It is always difficult, this explicit and uncensored recognition of our mortality.

More difficult was the next in line, my Grandma Green, known by adult friends and family as Gracie, a nickname for her beautiful first name, Grace. As a kid might assert, "She was the best grandma ever!" For a time, late in their lives, both grandparents moved to Topeka to be close to my parents and my uncle's family in Kansas City. They purchased a gingerbread house near my elementary school. Every day after school I'd rush to their tidy home, and Gracie would present me with delights such as homemade donuts and hot chocolate. She didn't just welcome me into her home; she also welcomed me into her heart. She loved me, and I knew it, and her love was deep and abiding and sustaining.

A few years later when I was in junior high school, and Grandpa Green had passed away, my father organized a road trip for the family. My sister, Julie, had married by that time and lived near Washington D.C., so our trip included plans to visit with Julie and her new husband. Before we got there, however, Dad drove us from Topeka all the way to eastern Canada and Maine and then down the east coast with stops in New York City and Atlantic City. Gracie and I occupied the back seat of the car, and during that time our relationship transcended from grand-parent/grandchild to becoming buddies. When my parents went to a Broadway show one night in New York, probably to get away from the buddies in the backseat, Gracie and I took on Times Square by ourselves and dined at a flashy Howard Johnson's, my favorite restaurant then. It was quite an adventure for both of us, and I felt almost as if a peer. For many years after that, my mother would joke about seeing the two of us walking purposefully through the hotel lobby on our way to tour the city, a resolute flash of independence and self-determination.

Not much more than a year later I heard some murmurings about Gracie's health. My parents remained hush-hush about the details other than to acknowledge she was sick. She spent some time in a Topeka hospital, and I remember once visiting her hospital room. She looked weak and gaunt and so very happy to see me, addressing me with her favorite pet name, "Honey Bug." I recall hugging her softly and sensing that she was gravely ill, but as barely a teenager, I had no words to attach to her situation, the clinical context of a diagnosis or prognosis. Back then, adults often assumed that children younger than high school age were ill-equipped emotionally and not ready to face uncensored medical diagnoses and prognoses.

Several days later my mother stopped me as I walked through our living room to inform me that Gracie had cancer. Mom was stoic and controlled, but I detected her restrained sadness. I didn't ask any questions because I didn't want to know any answers, and I traipsed upstairs to my bedroom. Mom stood at the bottom of the stairs, paused, and then announced the concluding fact of the situation: "Grandma Green is not going to get better."

I fell on my bed tearful and ashamed of crying since emotional boys back then were often chastised and labeled "cry babies." Plus, I was embarrassed to reveal this depth of emotion in front of my parents, and I assume they understood this in the way they informed me of Gracie's eminent death. She died a short time later, leaving a hole in my heart. I lost a grandmother who had made straight A's in her care, concern, and indulgences. She expressed her love and demonstrated her affection consistently throughout my childhood. She never asked anything of me in return.

So, Gracie's passing was my first experience of loss that was profound and lasting. Nobody could replace her, not even my mother's mother who appreciated me as her grandson but was too restrained to reveal actual affection except in indirect ways such as surprise treats from time to time. Gracie's passing left me also with other lingering nuances of loss: Was I worthy? Was I a good grandson? Did I fall short of her expectations? During some of my most precocious moments as a teenager, was I ever rude or ungrateful or demanding?

And so, those same questions have returned with the loss of others near and dear to me: sometimes a sense that maybe I did not measure up to their expectations, a concern that I could have been more giving, forgiving, and appreciative.

When I harbor these questions and feelings about loss, ancient and more recent, I am buoyed by a commencement address given by the late Steve Jobs, formerly CEO of Apple Computer and Pixar Animation Studios. He spoke to a 2005 graduating class of Stanford University about the stories of his struggles and successes, which included his thoughts about death and its meaning to arguably one of the greatest technology innovators of all time:

When I was 17, I read a quote that went something like: 'If you live each day as if it was your last, someday you'll most certainly be right.' It made an impression on me, and since then, for the past 33 years, I have looked in the mirror every morning and asked myself: 'If today were the last day of my life, would I want to do what I am about to do today?' And whenever the answer has been 'No' for too many days in a row, I know I need to change something.

Remembering that I'll be dead soon is the most important tool I've ever encountered to help me make the big choices in life. Because almost everything—all external expectations, all pride, all fear of embarrassment or failure—these things just fall away in the face of death, only leaving what is truly important. Remembering that you are going to die is the best way I know to avoid the trap of thinking you have something to lose. You are already naked. There is no reason not to follow your heart.

The great tech company leader then shared his clear view of choices and priorities, imparting valuable advice to young people with decades of opportunities still ahead of them:

No one wants to die. Even people who want to go to heaven don't want to die to get there. And yet death is the destination we all share. No one has ever escaped it. And that is as it should be because Death is very likely the single best invention of Life. It is Life's change agent. It clears out the old to make way for the new. Right now, the new is you, but someday not too long from now, you will gradually become the old and be cleared away. Sorry to be so dramatic, but it is quite true.

Your time is limited, so don't waste it living someone else's life. Don't be trapped by dogma—which is living with the results of other people's thinking. Don't let the noise of others' opinions drown out your inner voice. And most important, have the courage to follow your heart and intuition. They somehow already know what you truly want to become. Everything else is secondary.[23]

Thinking about my first significant loss also leads me to the present and future, as similar reflections will for most readers. Without debate, as we grow older we confront more frequent losses as a byproduct of the life-stage we are living. Older adults naturally lose more relatives, spouses, peers, friends, and associates than do younger people. Older adults also lose jobs, social status, relevance, and sometimes material wealth. Loss returns again and again as we progress toward the end of our lives, and, in some ways, our earliest experiences of great loss shape how we might react to new losses in the present and future. This fact of our existence—that with age comes more frequent losses— can be conceived as cloaked opportunities. Robert Weber Ph.D. and Carol Orsborn Ph.D. have written a terrific book that addresses spiritual growth in aging, entitled *The Spirituality of Age: A Seeker's Guide to Growing Older*. Through this thoughtful exploration of the intersection between aging and spiritual maturity, the authors examine three fundamental premises:

> (1) That spiritual growth and opportunity can come to us when we least expect it, whether we feel we are deserving of it or not; (2) that such moments of divine intervention can come about not only despite the challenges that aging has thrust upon us but because of them; and (3) that the Divine is both mysterious and loving.[24]

As we age, moving forward in life with greater spiritual growth can be augmented by looking back to rare moments when we have experienced

---

23 Jobs, Steve, 2005 Stanford Commencement Address, https://goo.gl/F1fo4C

24 Weber, Robert L. and Orsborn, Carol, *The Spirituality of Age: A Seeker's Guide to Growing Older*, published by Park Street Press, October 1, 2015, Kindle location 325

a sense of the Divine we do not encounter through our daily routines. These experiences can then take on new meaning as we discover insights that may have eluded us when young. Grandma Green's kitchen became the setting for one of my most intense memories of entering another dimension outside of everyday experience.

WHEN MY SPIRIT SOARED

I cherish a mystical world my mother created for my sister and me as we were growing up. Her love came to us through puppets and magic and fairytale stories and a fair amount of teasing. My earliest memories are chimerical flights into make believe.

One bright morning I was in Grandma Green's kitchen in Norton, Kansas. I was playing with my clown-like puppet, Happy, while mother entertained my sister, Julie, with another puppet, lavishly dressed in Victorian clothing, called Polly. Happy and Polly became childhood institutions for Julie and me—symbolic of the most comfortable world where all dreams come true.

Awhile later, Mom and Grandma towered above me, busily cooking while I played quietly on the linoleum floor. Growing bored with the puppet, I concentrated on Happy's candy cane-striped shoebox—the mottled cardboard walls and a musty smell as if a basement full of damp newspapers. Mother distracted me by pointing out two arch-shaped pieces of cardboard glued to the inside of the shoebox. She told me they were doors for Happy to escape to Never-Never Land when our family slept.

I stuck my head in the box and looked closely at those cardboard archways, trying to understand how this mystical transportation could occur. No light passed through them.

Suddenly, saffron sunlight streamed through the arches and for an unknown amount of time I was taken into a vision. My mother and grandmother remained behind and above me, perhaps amused with my careful analysis of the box, but I floated through those arches into a place full of light. They were behind me, immutable but not clearly visible. It could have been seconds or minutes, but through Happy's shoebox arches, I drifted into the infinite: golden sunshine, warmth, comforting mothers in checkered aprons, cheerful cherry pies, freedom from tired bodies, wisdom, and contentment.

From the other side of two Lilliputian arched doorways, I considered Grandma's kitchen and saw the familiar comfort of her polished domain, and I felt no fear. It was a floating feeling embraced by peace and acceptance. I was supposed to be there.

It is so easy for a rational adult to dismiss this childhood memory: perhaps a hallucination set free by speedy drugs poured into the system of an asthmatic child, or perhaps mingling of reality with a sleeping vision. There are many ways to explain away something that could not have happened.

There is also the possibility that I had passed through the boundaries confining human perception into a place where fantasy and reality are one. Grandma Green is cooking a perfect Sunday dinner for her son and daughter-in-law, and my vibrant, much younger mother is amusing herself by igniting the creativity of little souls, a place where Happy and Polly become living beings. Perhaps reality transformed long enough for me to embrace a perfect place where Grandma and Mom have now returned.

OTHER QUESTIONS TO CONSIDER ABOUT FIRST EXPERIENCES OF LOSS

Was your first loss of a loved one—such as a grandparent—your most challenging encounter with death? If not, why not?

Did you lose something besides a person that had an enormous impact on you, such as a toy, pet, or some other cherished object?

What did your first high-impact experience of loss teach you about the complicated feelings and thoughts associated with loss? Do those same feelings and thoughts return when you lose something or someone now?

Under what circumstances could a future loss resemble or resurrect your first sense of loss?

When you were very young, did you experience the loss of someone in a very profound and afflictive way whom you did not know personally, such as a celebrity or sports hero? Why was this person's death difficult for you?

CAN YOU EXPERIENCE THE PERSON YOU LOST OUTSIDE YOUR EGO?

SOCIAL PSYCHOLOGISTS HAVE identified "the spotlight effect" as significant to understanding how people tend to view themselves in a social context. The spotlight effect suggests that we often assume we are noticed more than we are. One facet of human existence is that most of us, most of the time, are in the center of our worlds. Each of us exists inside a body that experiences everything that happens to us in a very personal way, twenty-four hours a day, throughout our lifetime: each of us is the subjective see-ers, feelers, hearers, smellers, and tasters. Thus, we can be inaccurate in our understanding of how much others notice us, sometimes overestimating the degree to which people are paying attention and even caring what we are doing or saying, thinking or feeling.

Empirical research has demonstrated that drastic over-estimation of our effect on others is a common fragility in our social relations. This propensity to feel *under the spotlight* becomes especially prominent when we do something unusual, or something novel happens to us, such as experiencing the death of a loved one. One existential fact of life prevails over human existence: though we are at the center of our worlds, we are not at the center of everyone else's. We are unfolding stories bumping into other unfolding stories, and sometimes we wrongly assume that others are watching with critical judgment and exceptional focus on the details of our story. When they are not.

The "self-as-target bias" is closely related to the spotlight effect. This bias occurs when we believe that events are disproportionately directed toward us. For example, we may be involved in many aspects of our loved one's medical care before they pass. We may participate in medical appointments, run errands to pharmacies, and consult with professionals without our loved one's full and conscious participation. We may be forced to make difficult decisions. After our loss, we may start believing that our actions or lack of measures somehow contributed to the demise of our loved one. We feel guilty, second-guessing ourselves and focusing on how we might have failed our loved one. Self-doubt may haunt us.

Eckhart Tolle, best known as the author of *The Power of Now*, warns about the dangers of self-centered biases: "Because of its phantom nature, and despite elaborate defense mechanisms, the ego is very vulnerable and insecure, and it sees itself as constantly under threat. This, by the way, is the case even if the ego is outwardly very confident."[25]

Self-doubts hound us as unanswerable questions. Could I have asked more questions about treatment options earlier? Should I have asked the pharmacist about potential drug interactions? Was I assertive enough when requesting a second opinion? Did I fail to manage the situation with enough focus on details? Did I believe in the pronouncements of the wrong medical professional? Could I have done more? Said more? Given more?

Also, related to the spotlight effect is the "illusion of transparency," which is sometimes referred to as the observer's illusion of transparency. This bias involves the pervasive tendency to overestimate the degree to which our personal mental state—what we're feeling and thinking—is known and understood by others. Another facet of the illusion of transparency is an inclination for us to overestimate how well we understand others' internal mental states. This cognitive bias

---

25 Tolle, Eckhart, "*Practicing the Power of Now: Essential Teachings, Meditations, and Exercises from The Power of Now*, New World Library, Novato, California, Copyright 1999, page 28

is like the "illusion of asymmetric insight," in which we falsely believe our knowledge of the feelings and thoughts of others exceeds others' knowledge of us.

Professionals in the field of social psychology counsel us to be aware of the spotlight effect and related self-referential biases. Awareness of these human foibles can mollify the extent to which we believe we are in a social spotlight, and everyone is paying way too much attention to us. Then we can stop acting and feeling as if the whole world is watching and thus becoming overly self-critical of our actions. We can step out of the spotlight and begin the process of separating our subjective interpretations from objective facts of the situation.

One way to experience the person you have lost outside your ego involves letting go of the belief that this individual ever fully understood the many ways you think and feel. They may have known you well, but they could never step inside your head and fully grasp all your feelings about impending loss, your second-guessing about what to do or not to do as a caregiver, or your occasional unwelcome sense of anger, despair, loneliness, and impatience. Unless you verbalized these feelings in clear language to your loved one, and they were paying close attention while receiving your communications, they never completely understood how you felt, especially those feelings and beliefs that now might cause you some survivor's guilt or trepidation.

Further, as empathetic and as sensitive as you might have tried to be in this relationship, you probably never fully understood how your loved one felt as they went through the challenging experiences of sickness, decline, and suffering. You could not get inside their head and see the exact shape of things from the perspective of a dying person, the feelings of physical deterioration and the unsavory side effects of medical intervention and medications. Knowing that you could not know all there is to understand can liberate you from the responsibility to be prescient and fully informed as you go through difficult times of loss.

So, stripped of the illusion of being fully noticed and understood or completely understanding of the other person's point of view, we are left with what matters most: our *unconditional love* for the other person. With love as our priority, we can feel the person's presence and importance in ways language can never fully capture. We can recall our memories of them, unattached to guilt or wishful thinking. We can be assured that no matter what happened or how things turned out, we did what we had to do within the context of what we understood and could do. We accept, without further self-effacing judgment, our imperfections as humans but find comfort in the awareness that our love for the other person triumphs over our inherent humanity, our imperfections and limitations. Further, our love for the one we lost can evolve over time as we grow and change and gain a better understanding of the human condition—a state of existence commonly understood as *wisdom*. As time passes, we can grow in our ability to love the one we have lost, and this can supersede all our egotistical needs and natural human tendencies toward self-centeredness. "Whether life is worth living depends on whether there is love in life," opined psychiatrist and author R.D. Laing.

Gary Zukav, author of *The Seat of the Soul*, a *New York Times* best-selling book about spiritual growth, has written extensively about love between committed partners. He instructs: "Love is the ability to live your life with an empowered heart without attachment to the outcome, the ability within yourself to distinguish within yourself between love and fear and choose love regardless of what is going on inside yourself or outside. This is self-mastery or authentic power...that means you become clear, forgiving, humble and loving...you are grounded in harmony, cooperating, sharing and reverence for life."[26]

It is within our power to let go of internal debates over relationship baggage, our caregiving journey, our effectiveness, our patience, our intelligence, and our selflessness. We can let go of our ego's needs to be exceptional and relevant and right, understanding we can never be perfect within human relationships, but our love can transcend all this.

---

26 Zukav, Gary, as quoted on Goodreads.com, https://www.goodreads.com/author/quotes/26975

Our love can continue to grow for the person we have lost as we grow to understand ourselves better.

Buddha counseled that loving and letting go of someone outside your ego begins with loving yourself first. "You can search throughout the entire universe for someone who is more deserving of your love and affection than you are yourself, and that person is not to be found anywhere. You yourself, as much as anybody in the entire universe deserve your love and affection."[27]

---

27 Buddha, as quoted on Brainyquotes.com, https://goo.gl/fV2K4C

QUESTIONS TO CONSIDER ABOUT EGOLESS LOSS

How will you remember your loved one without self-doubts and feelings of unfinished business?

Do you believe your love can evolve even after your loved one has gone? How so?

If you could have one more conversation with your loved one, unimpeded by your former anxieties and concerns, how would that conversation proceed?

Can you accept and then dismiss the human shortcomings in the one you have loved and lost? Can you accept and then dismiss your shortcomings?

If our social reality tends to be clouded by self-referential biases, what have you learned from your loss that can help diminish your biases and their impact on future relationships?

HOW MUCH DO YOU
CONTEMPLATE YOUR DEATH?

I HAD BEEN rushed to the hospital perhaps minutes before suffocating from asthma. I was just five-years-old, and this moment was when I experienced the real possibility of my death. I did not understand death as an adult would, but I anticipated the possibility of going to heaven if I could no longer breathe. I was frightened and suspicious of everything going on around me. Although my father sat vigil near my hospital bed, I felt very alone and different from other kids my age. Asthma had imposed many restrictions on me. I could not play on bluegrass lawns during hot summer evenings; I could not go camping and sleep outdoors; I had a restricted diet, excluding my favorite staples such as wheat bread and chocolate. I knew I was weak compared to other kids my age, but I did not then appreciate the gravity of my thinness and comparatively stunted growth. Death lurked in that hospital room, and I was troubled by real nightmares that most children avoid confronting so head-on.

I write this to make clear that I began life contemplating my death long before most youngsters grasp the concept of death or their eventual termination as real and vivid. Since childhood, death has returned in other cloaks, beginning with the deaths of my grandparents. Those experiences made the abstraction of mortality more tangible, and like most people, when older relatives die we become more convinced of our impermanence, understanding we are in line eventually to cross over to the other side of life. Our place in line nudges to the front with each passing year and each death of a family member from older generations.

Most deceased members of my family have died of the diseases of aging, from heart disease to Parkinson's, to Alzheimer's disease, to cancer. Two notable deaths have clarified death, and therefore loss, from other perspectives.

My first cousin, Roberta, nicknamed Bobbi Kay, was the oldest of my six cousins, and she had a troubled life. She married young and gave birth to two daughters and sometimes seemed content within her family. She was also generous with her sense of humor and uncommon skills as a seamstress. Had she been born a few years later and been career motivated with proper direction from a wise adult mentor, she could have become a fashion designer. She often sewed clothes for my fashionable sister who appreciated our cousin's unique talents.

Back in the late 1960s, I desperately wanted a specific kind of shirt that was reminiscent of a Victorian era garb with billowy sleeves and a Henley-style collarless finish, a pullover, including a series of decorative buttons below the collar. Imagine the kind of shirt that Shakespeare's Romeo might have worn. The shirt was all the rage for cool young men, but it was nearly impossible to find a Henley pullover with billowy sleeves back then at traditional clothing stores. I sheepishly asked Bobbi Kay if she would consider making me a shirt of this style. I was then courting a beautiful and popular co-ed, and I felt extreme pressure to dress at the cutting-edge of sixties' fashion. Within a week, Bobbi Kay presented me with not one but two "Romeo shirts," as I called them for descriptive simplicity.

This small gesture was a huge gift in my mind because her Romeo shirts were as cool as I had ever seen. I received many compliments from peers, as well as a few jealous vibes, and my first major date with the alluring co-ed went very well as we attended a live "Chicago" concert in Kansas City. I was suitably dressed, and so was she. We connected through our smart fashion statements.

When I would call my cousin from time-to-time, she was always ready with a great joke or two, and her suburban life in Kansas City seemed normal enough. But my perception was not her reality.

Depression tortured her, and I'm reasonably sure that she had received some medical assistance through psychoactive medications. The first time she attempted suicide was not successful, and she appeared to be getting some help, especially from nurturing second cousins living in the area. But one day while her husband was working and her two daughters were at school, Bobbi Kay walked into her garage, closed all the doors tight, started her car, and eventually suffocated from carbon monoxide poisoning.

My sister, Julie, was most deeply affected by our cousin's suicide. They were close to the same age, had lived near each other in Kansas City, and had spent many years enjoying each other's company. When we received news of Bobbi Kay's suicide, Julie was coincidentally visiting me in Colorado Springs. Without hesitation, Julie picked up the telephone and called Bobbi Kay's oldest brother. To both of our shock and consternation, he was rude, treating Julie's call as if an insensitive intruder, although Julie honestly had hoped to offer sincere condolences to our cousins' parents, our aunt and uncle. This lack of empathy for someone's genuine sympathy was not uncommon in a dysfunctional relationship between our mother and her oldest brother. And not even in the context of a tragic death could condolences be received as genuine and meaningful.

Losing my cousin to suicide changed my relationship with death once again. First, she was an age peer who had been generous, funny, and well-liked by my sister and me. Up to that point, death was reserved for older family members who were "supposed to die" when their time came. Second, Bobbi Kay demonstrated through her suffering that psychic pain can be so unbearable; not even the love of her husband, daughters, and extended family members could ease her emotional burdens. I became aware that each of her survivors, all of us, have thought of our deaths and the possibility of ending it all when life carries too much weight and unhappiness. If Bobbi Kay, our affable, funny and talented cousin/wife/mother/daughter/sister could find no pathway to end her burdens other than suicide, then certainly self-annihilation could be a possible way out for any of her mourning family members.

Death is something healthy humans spend their lives trying to forestall through being safety conscious and maintaining the physical body by eating right, exercising, and finding a balance between work and leisure. Death is usually an uninvited intruder kept at bay until no other options remain. For a suicidal person, such as my cousin, the reality of death must become a welcome guest capable of delivering the sufferer from all the pain and disillusionment that life dishes out.

I now wish I had undertaken a more concerted effort to understand my cousin's life from her perspective. Since I studied psychology in college and worked for five years as a rehabilitation psychologist after graduate school, I had the knowledge and some of the tools to deliver therapeutic assistance if Bobbi Kay would have been willing to self-disclose with me. But by the time she descended into the morass of her psychic pain, I lived six-hundred miles away and was, as they say, "in a different world." I had left the field of psychology to pursue the rest of my career in advertising. We had not connected in years—again, somewhat driven by estrangement between her father and my mother—and so I had not thought of her much or concerned myself with occasional rumors that Bobbi Kay had become a very troubled cousin. Estrangement happens in a lot of extended families as children grow up and drift apart due to geography, career choices, and disaffection.

From 1972 to 1983, M*A*S*H was one of the most popular situation comedies on television. The storyline followed the staff of an army hospital during the Korean War as they helped the wounded and coped with extraordinary pressures through laughter, shenanigans, and pranks. Although set in Korea, the storyline followed closely with more contemporaneous political and social issues spawned by the Vietnam War.

As I contemplated the disconcerting realities of Bobbi Kay's demise, I listened to the theme song from M*A*S*H, aptly entitled, "Suicide Is Painless." The lyrics ring true and afflictive:

Through early morning fog I see
visions of the things to be
the pains that are withheld for me
I realize and I can see...

that suicide is painless
it brings on many changes
and I can take or leave it if I please.
I try to find a way to make
all our little joys relate
without that ever-present hate
but now I know that it's too late, and...

The game of life is hard to play
I'm gonna lose it anyway
The losing card I'll someday lay
so this is all I have to say.[28]

I wondered if Bobbi Kay had reached a point in her tortured life when she finally resigned herself to the futility of persisting and fighting depression and self-recrimination. One stanza rings especially poignant in the song lyrics: "The sword of time will pierce our skins / It doesn't hurt when it begins / But as it works its way on in / The pain grows stronger... watch it win."

With enough time passing, death comes to us all, and so I can understand the perspective of someone who may feel unrelenting psychic pain daily and then decide to end it all, quite correctly believing that pain will only grow more relentless and eventually win in the battle for life. Since I am her cousin, clearly there are facets to my struggles that invite reflection about the end of pain, the possibility that I too can end

---

28 "Suicide is Painless "(M.A.S.H Theme) - YouTube, http://www.youtube.com/watch?v=4gO7uemm6Yo (accessed July 20, 2016), words and music by Mike Altman, Johnny Mandel, arranged by Robert Schultz, copyright 1970

it all. I have never been close to taking my life, but I have looked squarely at the possibilities: how I might prefer to exit the stage, what I would communicate to those I love in the form of suicide notes, and how those most impacted might react. Is this not common at some point in most lives? Can it become life-affirming to spend some time considering and then rejecting the alternative?

The second death that added insight and weight to my understanding of death was an automobile accident that killed my sister's youngest daughter, Heather. She had been a beautiful and precocious child, the youngest of three children. Her middle name was Grace after her great-grandmother whom she never had an opportunity to meet. Her "Uncle Brent" was charmed from the beginning of her life in 1968 and determined to capture her beauty and delightful insouciance through photography. Heather usually became a willing accomplice and demonstrated an understanding of how to relate to my camera; together we created charming moments, capturing her growth and development from the toddler stage through her teen years. I was, of course, convinced that Heather "had the right stuff" to become a child model, and I nudged her without trying to become overly dictatorial about her future choices. An amateur photographer, I had confidence in my skills but reserved some doubt that I could ever be entirely objective about the modeling potential of my young niece.

My sister and brother-in-law relocated to San Francisco when Heather was around fourteen years old, and though "The City" has its many magical qualities, I remain convinced that it is not the best environment to raise young children. Heather soon began exploring the boundaries of acceptable behavior and meeting peers who influenced her to explore less healthy avenues. Her sense of independence, intelligence, and beauty may have buffered some of the negative influences that came her way, but nevertheless, she became wilder as she aged through her teens and into her early twenties, becoming a denizen of darkness, goth-garbed and sometimes eerie.

Our phone rang late one night interrupting a sound sleep. As I tried to wake up and return to full consciousness, Julie spoke on the other end of the line, informing me that Heather had been in a traffic accident. To my first groggy question concerning Heather's status, Julie told me with an anguished sadness that Heather had died. Julie asked me to come to San Francisco as soon as possible, and she said something to me that she had never spoken before that fateful night: "Brent, *I need you...*"

After arriving in San Francisco, the following day, I began helping our family manage the emotional impact of what had happened, learning more details about the traffic accident and who was at fault, and determining what we could do about an injustice that had become Heather's fate. A dark storm gathered above our small family as we came to terms with the facts of the accident and decided how we would stage a farewell event for Heather Grace. Being a writer who sometimes finds consolation and understanding through the clicking of a computer keyboard, I began writing about Heather's final day and her impact on our lives:

A GARLAND FOR HEATHER

San Francisco coffee house somewhere on Courtland Street near Bernal Heights. The hum of activity around me: steam gurgling through low-fat milk, people wearing faded denim, in line and out, easy going but rushing, a rustling *Chronicle* in the hands of a middle-aged man sitting next to me. Now black ink covers his fingertips. On this day, my niece soils his fingers.

I imagine: Take Heather's obituary on page C-11 times a few million Sunday morning fingers—all probing for connection with the ambiguous, often indifferent world. Many are touching Heather, knowing something of her, but only a few grasp the three hundred words that summarize her brief life. It comes down to three hundred words, plus or minus a few, to render this enigmatic young woman into a neat, comprehensible package, her quest for celebrity now carbon smudging fingers, turning pages, a few stopping long enough to notice the salient facts: 28 years old, loved animals, must have been a beauty, dressed smartly. Maybe a common conclusion creeps around *The City*: young, much too young—tragic.

Heard about that awful mid-day car accident on Highway 4 near Martinez. She was the passenger and only fatality, wasn't she? Could there have been alcohol involved? Drugs? More carnage littering highways, jamming traffic. When are we going to slow down?

But for the cheap printer's ink smudging fingers, this is a pristine day—a bright, dry, spring-in-bloom Sunday, a day full of possibilities, of choices. For most denizens of this coffee house, there is nothing close to closure; they/we have so many options, whether a slow stroll through Golden Gate Park or to sip coffee in a dark nook, warmed by a single bulb and a good book.

Her body touches darkness now—her spirit? Who is clear? But her body is cold, still, shrouded in the blackness she chose to honor during that Goth phase, but there is now no movement from it—can't be—no more compression of determination left to transform hope. No way for her to move to another temporary, shadowy place, to change this day, this week, with the flowing mélange of a searching life.

Her impact was much more than three hundred words. She could reach into your psyche, own it, possess it, and then abruptly release it. Whoever stood up to the challenge must eventually withdraw, changed, chastened—contemplative. Heather was never just here: she was HERE. In your face. Pulling down your defenses and, as if a piercing arrow, finding your heart, making you crave for a way to tether diffident love; making you pray for a breakthrough in her journey to unite body, mind, and spirit; making you want to hand her fulfillment, while helping her shift uncommon allure into achievement. She always could have had it all, yet for reasons mostly unclear, she chose to possess little—save the yearnings of so many hearts and a few orphaned pets.

But I cannot push away her power to retreat: It was the wellspring of so much trepidation among those who loved her. Her armor often dulled the precision of her exuberant love. It was the pain of people, unreliable at best, insensitive at worst, that undercut this vulnerable soul. Her sensitivity, her yearning for predictable people, conversely pushed her into escape velocity. Love and fear of us hung her life in suspended animation. She could give us access, but not too much, access, but not enough. That was Heather.

And quite possibly, the dialectic between loving/needing people and fearing/shunning them brought her to animals. They, more than we, could count on Heather. Lesser creatures could return what we cannot: unconditional love, dependent appreciation, no aspirations for her but to let her be, to let her feed and caress and manage. Furry people gave us the clearest view of her, who among them was unfettered by suspicion, longing, or unanswered expectations.

So, the newspaper carrying the framework of Heather's life will become waste tomorrow, to be tossed into landfills, or recycled, or gather dust in garages and attics. Smudged fingers will be washed. Our family will cleanse itself, thinking mostly about the sublime moments that were her best and brightest hours. We, too, will discard the boxed words trying to contain her life—save a few clippings—but we, unlike the reading man next to me and all the strangers out there, will wonder what could have become of her. Such fleeting chances she had, our Heather. She was much, much more than so many fingertips darkened with the ink of her once-upon-a-time passage among us.

Footnote: On March 6, 1997, Heather Grace Luttjohann died in a multi-car accident on Highway 4 near Martinez, California, an infamous, crowded, high-speed deathtrap.

Heather required me to look at death, not just as the conclusion to an octogenarian's long life or as the rescuer from unrelenting pain in someone much younger who could not cope with existence—an older cousin choosing suicide over survival—but rather Heather's demise demanded me to accept that death waits for everyone and spares nobody. Death gets to choose the time, means, and context for each life to end. Heather was twenty-eight-years-old, had most of her life in front of her, and was beginning to mature out of her most impetuous years. She was a star in the making from the perspective of her uncle, and she was just starting to appear quite capable of creating a fruitful and productive life. Then … wham, a driver of a car in which she was a passenger turned into oncoming highway traffic. Two vehicles hit the side of this car at full highway speed, and blunt force traumas were too extensive for Heather to survive.

I have wondered if she suffered and if she had any level of consciousness as internal bleeding drained her life away. Did she understand what had happened to her and perhaps had a few moments to think about those she had loved? Did she know in her heart how much she had been loved by her mother, father, stepfather, sister, brother, uncle, and aunt? Did she exit this life through the tunnel so often described by those who have had near-death experiences? Did she see a light at the end of the passageway that was a signpost of God calling? Would she eventually find her great-grandparents and grandparents on the other side and in doing so also receive the promises of resurrection and salvation?

Looking at death can be life-affirming. It doesn't need to mire us in thoughts of uselessness, nihilism, self-recrimination, and indifference to the future. Just a reminder that our days are numbered invites us to consider our blessings, strengthen our resolve to carry on, and escalate our compassion for all creatures, great and small. Many daily annoyances and temporary setbacks lose the power to deter us from a path—any path—forward. We can become more grateful for those who have gone before us as each has taught us unique ways to adapt to the days, week, months, and sometimes years involved in passing on.

King Solomon addressed the essential nature of life and death and the choices we have between our beginning and ending:

To everything there is a season and time to every purpose under
heaven;
A time to be born and a time to die…
A time to kill, and a time to heal;
A time to break down, and a time to build up;
A time to weep and a time to laugh,
A time to mourn, and a time to dance,
A time to keep, and a time to let go…[29]

My Grandma Green left quietly, never bothering me with her pain or
litany of losses as her body gave out. My mother never complained about
the ravages of Parkinson's disease, a debilitating disease keeping her
imprisoned in a nursing home for over four years, while also once being
the victim of mistreatment by a nurse's aide charged with her care. My
father protested his waning physical limitations a bit more, but he, too,
prepared well for the final weeks of his life when he tried to become
rehabilitated but then accepted that medical science could provide no
more rescues. My sister endured uncertainties of lung cancer, discomforts of chemotherapies, and a harsh existential awareness that many
of her plans for retirement and travel would never come to fruition. My
cousin took "the easy way out" and in so doing demonstrated another
facet of humanity's free will: the awesome power that comes with a decision not to exist any longer, to self-terminate. My niece left us with the
promises and possibilities of youth still present. She had been pursu-
ing a career taking care of animals and seeing possibilities that her life
could mean something and have value for others in need. Her life ended
just short of her opportunity to self-actualize her dreams.

Death was the one constant connecting all these human stories together. The outcome of physical death is always the same: an end to
existence and decomposition of the body, either by natural means or
by cremation. But the final chapter of life is uniquely different just as

---

29 Ecclesiastes 3 KJV - To everything there is a season https://www.biblegateway.com/
passage/?search=Ecclesiastes+3&version=KJV (accessed July 20, 2016).

we are unique humans. This means we have choices. This means I have choices. This means you have choices.

Elizabeth Edwards, wife of former 2004 Democratic vice-presidential nominee and U.S. Senator from North Carolina, John Edwards, died in 2010, a provocative public death as a breast cancer victim. She wrote poignantly about choices we have as mortal humans: "The days of our lives, for all of us, are numbered. We know that. And yes, there are certainly times when we cannot muster as much strength and patience as we would like. It's called being human. But I have found that in the simple act of living with hope, and in the daily effort to have a positive impact in the world, the days I do have are made more meaningful and precious. And for that I am grateful."[30]

---

30 Edwards, Elizabeth, as quoted on Goodreads.com, http://www.goodreads.com/quotes/tag/life-and-death

QUESTIONS TO ASK WHEN CONTEMPLATING DEATH

Do you find any peace in knowing that you will die, or does the end of life provide a disagreeable sense of foreboding?

Which person close to you had the greatest impact on your understanding of death and why?

Do you want to take an active role in planning your death and its aftermath, or would you rather leave that to others?

We all feel pain when someone close to us dies, but do you feel empathy for the deaths of others you do not know? How about the deaths of prison inmates through executions?

Do you have the words and wisdom to help a child understand and accept death?

IS SUICIDE PAINLESS?

HE WAS WEALTHY, internationally acclaimed, and creatively prolific, a celebrity who set many acting benchmarks. Then at age 63 he killed himself by hanging, and it remains difficult to understand why.

Robin Williams, a beloved comic genius, earned many accolades including an Academy Award, three Grammys, and five Golden Globes. His acting range covered an endearing extraterrestrial in the 1970's hit television sit-com *Mork & Mindy* and an Oscar-winning performance as Dr. Sean McGuire, a circumspect psychotherapist in the film *Good Will Hunting.*

Depression has been the most popular explanation for Williams' suicide. Depression is a brain disease, a biochemical misalignment, a mood disorder. Depression has been described as a dark tunnel, a state of aching sadness in which the afflicted person can no longer see liberating possibilities for brighter, happier days.

And while this explanation renders the loss of such a magnetic personality less mystifying, a psychological disorder may not fully contain self-destruction of this magnitude. Though Robin must have been depressed and felt socially isolated, what other psychic nightmares haunted Robin? What was Robin Williams thinking and feeling in the months, days, and hours before he hanged himself?

It behooves suicide experts to look beyond brain chemistry. Perhaps Williams, like other male peers who have self-terminated, may have finally reached a point of no return because of the socio-cultural context in which he lived. That background includes his generational affiliation and status as a post-sixty man.

Williams was born in 1951 and thus a member of the Baby Boomer generation. He grew up in times of ebullient optimism, a post-World War era of unbounded possibilities. During his two years at the prestigious Julliard School, he must have sensed the seismic power of his massive generation, a collective consciousness that bowled through the prejudices and predictabilities of older generations. So, is it a leap to conclude that Williams, like millions of his peers, had enormous expectations?

In a pivotal book entitled *Great Expectations: America and the Baby Boom Generation,* author Landon Y. Jones, formerly managing editor of *People* magazine, coined the label "Baby Boomers" and helped propel this generation toward the focal point of American culture. One popular generational narrative goes something like this: Boomers were given unprecedented abundance by their parents, the tireless, self-sacrificing GI Generation. Boomers can expect great things to happen throughout life: stellar education, brilliant careers, economic security, satisfying soul mates, and material acquisitions that ameliorate occasional setbacks.

Unmet dreams early in life can foment pessimistic assessments later. Recent research by David Blanchflower and Andrew Oswald confirms that the proverbial mid-life crisis—the least happy time of life—arrives between age 45 and 65, with males skewing older. Further, the business of "life review" is relative. A dazzling career and superior status to most observers may seem doggedly unsatisfying to an actor on the implacable stage of reality.

Higher than any other age group, suicide rates for Boomers rose 40 percent from 1999 through 2011, according to the Centers for Disease Control and Prevention.[31] Williams was far from alone in his decision to self-terminate.

---

31 Elinson, Zusha, "Robin Williams's Age Group at Heightened Suicide Risk," Wall Street Journal, August 12, 2014: https://goo.gl/1lsnTy

We are left wondering which of Williams' high expectations remained unmet. What might he have wished for that he had not achieved? Confidence in a future as luminous as his celebrated past? Freedom from addiction? Self-acceptance? Anonymity?

Added to the burden of oversized generational hopefulness could have been the weight of maleness. Son of a GI Generation father, Williams may have also learned that a man is what he does, not necessarily who he is. A man is a doctor, engineer, pastor, or actor. Maleness is concrete, specific, and unwavering toward the goal of external achievement. And for some men, the goalpost never stops moving farther downfield.

Even for those who choose the Occam's razor explanation—that depression was the culprit—there may be another possibility: andropause or "male menopause." Some authorities believe that reduction of the male hormone testosterone in middle-aged men can trigger depression and suicidal tendencies.

According to Jed Diamond, Ph.D., author of *Male Menopause* and *Irritable Male Syndrome*, andropause is a hormonal change in middle-aged men that has potentially devastating physical, psychological, interpersonal, social, sexual, and spiritual aspects. With these changes sometimes come insurmountable challenges of coming to terms with aging, and statistics confirm the perilous consequences of growing old a male.

"There is a silent health crisis," observes Dr. Diamond, "with males living sicker than females and dying from fourteen of the top fifteen leading causes of death at rates higher than those for women." Eighty percent of all suicides in the U.S. are men. The male suicide rate at midlife is three times higher than the rate for women. As men age over 65, the suicide rate accelerates like a speeding bullet to seven times higher.[32]

In his portrayal of John Keating, the beloved English teacher in the acclaimed coming-of-age movie, *Dead Poets Society*, Williams stood on a

---

32 Diamond, Jed, A Grand Rounds Webinar for Men and the Women Who Love Them," as described on MenAlive.com: http://menalive.com/grand-rounds/

school desk and asked his students why he would do this. To feel taller? No.

"I stand upon my desk," he announced, "to remind myself that we must constantly look at things in a different way."

He was a resounding voice of a generation. He won acclaim for his abilities to interpret the human condition in ways that made us laugh at ourselves. And so, we are left questioning when he stopped seeing things in a different way, whether blinded by a tunnel of depression or high expectations dashed by sobering maturity. Or perhaps from being a man growing older, another Boomer male suffering an aching sigh of diminishing self-worth.

Whatever psychological burdens took Robin Williams and his comic genius from us, we can rest assured he would have had some ironic twist on the harsh reality of his final month, weeks, and days.

"Reality: What a concept!"

I SHALL NOT BE AGING BY BRENT GREEN

I have seen glowing daylight fading,
Into that good dark night waiting,
As Mom, Dad, Sis and one dear friend,
Have gently shown me how this will end.

I have seen a solstice scores of times,
And paid my dues for several climbs,
While making the fleeting choice of life,
To confront a dare of everlasting strife.

I shall not be aging, merely rearranging,
I shall not be aging, only captivating,
I shall not be aging, simply elevating.

My hikes along the roads not taken,
Have discovered a man unforsaken,
The same soul who has taken it all,
The one who has answered his call.

Freedom is another word for aging,
When all that I am is still raging,
Yet my heart is tenderly fulfilled,
The best I could do, my fear now stilled.

I shall not be aging, merely motivating,
I shall not be aging, only innovating,
I shall not be aging, simply cultivating.

So let the hours, days and years fly by,
The man who sees inside shall never die,
My memory will live through eternity,
When all that ever was becomes Unity.

QUESTIONS TO REFLECT UPON ABOUT SUICIDE

*Have you ever considered suicide, and if so, what led
you to this possibility for self-termination?*

*What brought you back from the brink, and
could your realizations help others?*

*Is suicide a coward's way out, or can self-termination
be a reasonable decision for some who cannot find happiness, self-acceptance, and satisfaction?*

*If you could have spoken with Robin Williams, what would
you have said to discourage him from committing suicide?*

*Can the possibility of our power to commit suicide any time we
choose strengthen us and help us endure suffering better?*

CAN LETTING GO BECOME BRINGING IN?

RODNEY WILSON HAD been a high school classmate, a big guy with a voluminous voice and more than his share of adolescent pimples. I recall he laughed a lot. His wit and upbeat personality ensured his popularity in a cliquey high school at a time when the social norm required students to be standoffish, judgmental, and restrained. Rodney never seemed to judge his classmates as to their worthiness for social interaction, and he treated everyone with genuine warmth. Rodney loved his peers, and they returned his spontaneous ardor with heaps of goodwill. I never got to know him well, nor did we become close friends, but I felt at ease around him when our paths periodically intersected around our high school campus. He was the kind of kid who would inspire smiles, not caution, in others.

Rodney died in Vietnam in 1969. The details of his death did not survive his passing. I learned of his demise many months later while I was attending college at the University of Kansas. I had been opposed to that conflict, as had most college students at KU, and Rodney's death added a face and name to my conviction that Vietnam was a senseless, undeclared war, a brutal conflict the United States should never have pursued. (I am writing this passage, ironically, while wearing a new shirt I purchased at Costco, manufactured in—you guessed it, Vietnam.)

I recall feeling sad to learn about Rodney's death, but I did not take time when I was a college student fully to consider the implications of his death or the deeper meaning to me. I heard the news back then, gave it some passing consideration, felt sadness for his heroic sacrifice, and then moved on with my young life. Rodney became one footnote, most significantly because he was the only high school classmate who had added one more name to a list of 58,000 American killed-in-action casualties of that war.

Fast forward thirty years. Our thirtieth high school graduation class reunion in 1997 arrived too early in the evolution of internet adoption for many classmates to possess email addresses, so the anniversary marking three decades since graduation had been organized with mailed notices, as had been all reunions before 1997. We typically received a few mailed notices from our reunion organizing committees. Thus the committee sent a "save the date" postcard, a formal invitation letter, and then a follow-up reminder postcard. Ten years later, in 2007, a few of my most spirited high school classmates again busily organized our fortieth anniversary reunion. But for the first time in the history of these decennial class gatherings, organizational communication about the reunion relied more on email than U.S. mail. Instead of a handful of communications, sparingly mailed, digital floodgates opened, and we started receiving regular communications from the organizing committee and another dozen or so prolific email communicators.

Email made run-up to the fortieth reunion uniquely different because we started experiencing a reunion before a reunion by connecting and catching up with myriad email messages. Many emails were frivolous in tone, themed around fun and nostalgic remembrances. Some were all business such as requests to help find missing classmates and locate their email addresses. A popular athlete and scholar from my class, who eventually became a psychology department chair at a major university, began courting our senior class president, an intelligent and connected woman who had become the first female in our high school's history to hold the ultimate class leadership office. (These two divorcees eventually reconnected offline and married, a triumph of relinking and nostalgia.) Email gave class members a new way of deepening the reunion experience since we learned more about each other's lives, and of course, some class members also renewed childhood friendships offline.

Two years earlier, in 2005, I had been invited to be a guest speaker for the organizing committee of the White House Conference on Aging. This honor and opportunity brought me to Washington D.C., and I extended my stay in the nation's capital for an extra day to visit popular landmarks and memorials. I fixated on one memorial above all others.

The Vietnam War Memorial Wall spans 246 feet and nine inches, consisting of gabbro walls etched with names of fallen servicemen, presented as panels erected in horizontal rows. The walls have been sunken into the earth with backfill piled up behind them. At the memorial's apex, dark onyx-colored walls intersect at a vertical height of 10.1 feet. Symbolically, this unusual architectural design has been described as a wound, closed and healing.

When I gazed at the wall for the first time, I saw my reflection simultaneously peering back through engraved names, which Maya Lin, the memorial's young Asian architect, intended symbolically to bring the past and present together (fallen servicemen's names as witnessed by gazing, living survivors). One wall points toward the Washington Monument and the other aims in the direction of the Lincoln Memorial. Each wall has seventy-two panels with seventy listing names and two blank panels at the extremities. A path meanders along the base of the Wall. I strolled along this perimeter for at least an hour while consumed by somber reflections about that divisive war and its impact on my life as an impressionable college student.

The Wall has exactly 58,307 names, as of May 2015, including eight women. Bewildered and dazed by the enormity of so many faceless names etched in black monolithic walls, I finally consulted a directory located on a nearby podium so I could find one important name representing unresolved feelings: Rodney's name. A few minutes later I discovered his name etched into black stone.

Grief permeates the area. Grandchildren become curious and rein in their hyperactivity. Some silent visitors leave flowers and mementos for the fallen then disappear. I became transported. Seeing Rodney's etched name changed my relationship with his memory and sacrifice. This symbolic encounter with a past life became palpable, ragged, depressing, and affirming all at once. I silently prayed with whispers for his immortal soul and thanked him for his sacrifice. I took several digital photos to capture these fleeting memories. I had no plan then for my photos other than as mementos of my visit to the Wall, to be tucked away on my computer's hard drive and probably never to be seen by others.

As a flurry of emails between my classmates continued in anticipation of our fortieth-class reunion, during one thoughtful and emotional day I decided to dispatch an email with the subject line: *The Wall.* I also attached my digital photo of Rodney's name etched on the Vietnam Memorial Wall.

My cover note came jarringly to the point:

Dear TWHS classmates,

Rodney Wilson was just one of 58,000 Americans killed in Vietnam, and he was one of us. The enemy shot him on July 3, 1969. He would have turned 58 on September 28, 2007.

Although it is fun to revisit bygone times, and maybe rediscover some old and dormant feelings about former classmates and shared experiences, I can't help but become reflective about this reunion.

Philip Roth, a Pulitzer-prize winning author of *American Pastoral,* wrote these thoughts about his 45th high school reunion:

It's astonishing that everything so immediately visible in our lives as classmates we still remember so precisely. The intensity of feeling that we have seeing one another is also astonishing. But most astonishing is that we are nearing the age that our grandparents

were when we first went off to be freshmen. What is astonishing
is that we, who had no idea how anything was going to turn out,
now know exactly what happened. That the results are in for
the class of (1967)—the unanswerable questions answered, the
future revealed—is that not astonishing? To have lived—and in
this country and in our time, and as who we were. Astonishing.[33]

Sharing the photo of Rodney is my way of expressing gratitude just to have an opportunity to attend a 40th class reunion. When another 40 years passes, odds are most of us will be gone (although we Boomers will populate the ranks of centenarians as no generation has before us: 2.1 million by 2065).

I'm looking forward to seeing you and our other classmates.

Brent

This email and its attached photo caused more reactions than any other email sent about the reunion across a span of six months. Some gasped, I am sure. Others felt the big guy's presence and missed him in a new way from the distance of forty years. Many responded with their group emails by sharing reminiscences and a sense of loss. Some dispatched private notes thanking me for injecting a dose of reality into some of the more feckless chitchats and teasing that prior emails had inspired. Several other classmates acknowledged that they, too, had visited the Vietnam War Memorial and taken the time to find Rodney's name. One classmate had even made a charcoal rubbing of his name. A few email lurkers, who had not yet responded to any emails about the forthcoming class reunion, stepped out of the digital shadows and reintroduced themselves to their classmates.

I became surprised and gratified to see my email about Rodney stimulate a tribal reaction that we had never accomplished before as a group: We mourned Rodney's passing as a class, something we had

---

33 Chapter 2 - Philip Roth's American Pastoral, http://americanpastoral.wikidot.com/chapter-2 (accessed July 20, 2016).

failed to do during any of the previous reunions. The thought had not occurred to anyone, and perhaps our typical weekend reunion experiences earlier in life had not provided the right context for such somber reflections. Two-day reunions, held so infrequently, demanded focus on fun and frivolity.

My story about Rodney is all about letting go by bringing in. Rather than allowing him to remain a distant memory within the community that knew him best—thus immaterial in the present tense—my *The Wall* email made his passing real and palpable and relevant. The jovial kid deserved to be remembered by all our classmates. He earned the honor of being acknowledged: he had sacrificed his life in a war that still arouses raucous divisiveness. Many of us brought back buried memories and thus embraced the thoughts and feelings that caused us pain and conflict during that distant chapter of American history. In the conception articulated by VITAS chaplain Mark McGann, who I introduced with this book's Preface, we *embraced grief* four decades after our loss of a valued classmate. Embracing these feelings and memories also gave us a way to let go...finally.

The photo and cover email also became my symbolic gesture of saying goodbye in more of a complete way than would have occurred had Rodney's return from Vietnam in a body bag concluded with a memorial and burial service. Too few would have made it to a service. Many of us were not then emotionally ready to process his death in such a personal way, given all the vitriol about Vietnam taking place on college campuses throughout the nation at the time of his death.

Bringing in the emotionally and historically relevant facts of Rodney's sacrifices and heroism is also a way of releasing burdens some of us carry at some times. Other classmates also had been drafted and served, although they returned home alive and well if not damaged psychically by the cultural disaster of Vietnam. Some had never mourned his passing, either for lack of timely news about his death or because they had been far removed from class news; they had never been so directly confronted until they saw his name etched into the Wall. Perhaps other classmates never felt connected to their high school experience because of social isolation, abject rejection, or other failures to measure up to peer standards during high school. Rodney's unfortunate death—the first member of our class to die after high school—could offer a meaningful connection back to the high school years, mollifying feelings of exclusion and irrelevance that troubled them when still teenagers.

Letting go in this context means settling accounts and finally moving on.

My high school was in Topeka, Kansas, geographically situated in the epicenter of upper-middle-class neighborhoods populated by wealthy and successful professionals and entrepreneurs. Most of my peers never worried about their fate following high school, even with the military draft looming like a dark thunderstorm over our ascension into higher education and eventually careers. Most of the male high school graduates had college student draft deferments in their plans. For whatever reasons, either reticence to attend college or the call of foreign adventures that inspire some enlistees, Rodney chose military service over higher education. He was clearly intelligent enough to succeed in college had he chosen that path, but instead, he became a soldier in Vietnam. Some of his male peers may have felt a modicum of guilt for not being eager to serve since most of us are sons of GI Generation fathers who served during World War II. We grew up believing that military service is heroic though sometimes tragic in consequences. We watched blockbuster movies that glorified military heroes, and one of the first U.S. presidents that any of us could remember was General Dwight David Eisenhower, a fellow Kansan, who had been Supreme Commander of the Allied Forces in Europe. Boy Scouts further inculcated implicit and honored values of courage, self-sacrifice, preparedness to defend the nation, absolute joys of adventure, and righteousness of patriotic service.

Part of me also wanted to fight and serve, as my father had—so much so that I signed up for Reserved Officer Training Corps

(ROTC) during my first year at the University of Kansas. I was becoming less and less convinced that I wanted to be a foot soldier in Vietnam, given the bellicose anti-Vietnam War movement that had been growing more vociferous on the nation's college campuses. But assuming I must eventually serve after college graduation once I was no longer protected with a student deferment (and that's the way things looked when I started college), I concluded that the best way for me to participate in a war would be as an officer. However, I grew up with severe bronchial asthma, and it took just a few weeks for an ROTC instructor to advise me that I could not qualify for officer's training due to my medical history. A diagnosis of chronic asthma ended my internal debate to serve or not to serve, but it did not end my psychological negotiations about the nobility or foolishness of being an American soldier deployed to Vietnam and the nation's most unpopular war. I never truly resolved the grating ambiguity of military service in my life, and in the lives of others close to me, until I experienced catharsis when finding Rodney's name on the Vietnam Wall, remembering him from a fresh perspective, and sharing his memory with my classmates.

I assume that "letting go by bringing in" also created an indelible release for peers who graduated with me from high school. We embraced our shared grief, and I believe this led to a class catharsis, expressed through email communications. I judge this to be true because of private emails sent to me from those who had received my Wall photograph and email concerning Rodney, for example:

David wrote back:

I had some dreams about him in the early years after he died that were very powerful. I always felt like they were more than just dreams. There are many kinds of dreams, but I had a few dreams where he appeared, and it was really like a communion of souls to me, a sort of healing. Of course, anyone can take any view they want on things like that, but I felt like there was some real connection, across whatever barriers of space and time there were there.

Steve (also a Vietnam vet) wrote back:

Over the past years, I've traveled back to Washington DC several times. On my first visit after The Wall was erected, I paid a solemn visit. Setting aside my "brothers in arms" who gave their lives fighting in South Vietnam, I went immediately to Rodney's inscription. The tears started at that point and continued as I visited the many inscriptions for Marines I had served with from September 1968 to October 1969. Strong, brave and bright. That's how I remember Rodney.

Sara, president of our senior class, wrote back:

This beautiful picture of yours certainly struck a chord with a lot of people from our class. I was thinking last night that Rodney might have been very surprised at how many people have such fond and funny memories of him. (I remember him letting me sneak into the movies at, I think, the Jayhawk Theater, where he was working!) Thanks for starting this.

Marsha wrote back:

I don't know why, but for all these years, I always remembered that Rodney Wilson had died in the Vietnam War. I too found his name when I visited The Wall several years ago. I happened to be there on Memorial Day and went there only to find myself overwhelmed with uncontrollable emotion. It is so amazing the impact this memorial has on one. Great picture. It makes one stop to think about all that has happened in these last 40 years of life. My son-in-law is currently in Iraq, so this is all near and dear to my heart.

Carl wrote back:

Thanks for reminding all of us that we have lost some magnificent old friends. I used to walk around Rodney's neighborhood with him on weekend evenings as we both attempted to be the toughest, coolest guys in town. Rodney always worked the edge of "acceptable behavior," and that made him a lot of fun to be around. He knew how to disconnect the odometer on my parents' car so that we could take long car trips to Kansas City, Ottawa and elsewhere to meet up with girls Rodney had met somewhere. We would drive all night, and my parents would check the numbers and congratulate me for driving only eight miles, to and from some extremely acceptable chaperoned event. Rodney could have been an excellent athlete had he chosen to participate. You will recall that he had a very muscular, athletic body. He was always challenging me to arm wrestling contests! Rodney was cool then, and he would be cool now. But behind his bravado, was a warm, loyal guy. I can still see his photo in the newspaper after he had been killed in Vietnam. What a shame that Rodney and so many young soldiers lost their lives and devastated families and friends with each tragic incident.

Sam wrote back:

About 15 years ago, I took my family to Washington DC and visited The Wall as well. I did a pencil tracing of Rodney's name. I thought it was inspiring and sad at the same time. It was soundless, and the reflective quality of The Wall says a lot about those inscribed there and us. Rodney was a neat guy, and I do think about him from time to time.

Before this momentous email to my high school classmates, the subject of Rodney had never been examined as a group. He had not been acknowledged and remembered. His relevance became clearer to some of those who had forgotten him or never had thought actively about his death.

Being imprinted on the Vietnam Memorial Wall, Rodney's name gave me a misty sense of pride, knowing that although his death was tragic, he is permanently part of an engraved memorial in our nation's capital, a place of great honor and respect and reverence. Though he lived for just nineteen years, his name is now a substantial part of the historical record for as far into the future as we can imagine, a form of achievement that no other classmate can claim. He is one of us; he represents our best intentions: courage, sacrifice, love of country, a personification that "freedom isn't free." In death, he is part of something greater than he had been as just another army draftee from Kansas. Indirectly, this makes his classmates and friends part of something larger through our memories and shared respect.

With this unprecedented exchange of explicit emails, we could let Rodney go as we never had before, but with the assurance that he will never be forgotten as long as any of us who knew him are still alive. We brought him into our contemporary virtual community by considering his living years once again, by learning things about him that all of us did not know, and by sharing feelings beyond memories: a loss that comes with a peer's untimely death and a sense of loss when considering our eventual demise as well.

And, perhaps privately, some of my high school classmates took another look at their mortality because facing the death of a peer, even forty years after his death, invites us to consider our ultimate passing. We can *let go* by *bringing in* the universal fact of our existence: we too shall end. Chaplain Mark McGann believes that our death is the greatest grief each of us must face.

Jane E. Brody, the former personal health columnist and science writer for *The New York Times*, examined the choices we have when confronting our death through her impressive *Times* magazine article entitled, "Facing Your Own Mortality":

Intellectually, we all know that death is a fact of life. But most people tend to avoid thinking about their mortality, especially when they are young. For healthy young people, death seems so remote. But with a life-threatening experience—a serious illness, for example, or an accident—the confrontation is upon them. Anger, depression or panic are typical responses. But some people, young and old alike, remain calm when death suddenly presents itself, and this calmness may, on occasion, be lifesaving. People who have begun to develop a sound philosophy of life, and the lust for life that grows out of it, seem best able to stay calm when the image of death flashes on the horizon. [34]

---

34 Brody, Jane E., "Facing Your Own Mortality," as written by the former personal health columnist and a science writer for *The New York Times*, first published October 9, 1988: https://goo.gl/zRqpSc

QUESTIONS TO THINK ABOUT CONCERNING LETTING GO BY BRINGING IN

Has anyone from your past died but you have not fully contemplated the meaning of their passing?

How have you processed the grief of your death, the extinction of your personality and all your memories?

What steps can you take today to finish saying good- bye to someone you have loved and lost?

Which celebrity death has affected you the most and why?

What can you share with others, such as school class- mates, concerning the passing of a shared friend?

AFTER LOSS, WOULD YOU DESCRIBE YOUR CHARACTER DIFFERENTLY?

THE DISTURBING NEWS first came as an oddball ploy. I thought the teacher had invented the story to manipulate my classmates and me into appreciating history as something more than irrelevant facts and dates. He was an imaginative educator and relished making the past come alive for self-absorbed adolescents. I did not stop then to consider how unkind a pedagogical ruse that would be and therefore unacceptable.

So, okay, the president has been shot.

I was sitting in a prefab annex, a temporary classroom, one other way my junior high school coped with a tsunami of Baby Boomers overwhelming facilities. The feeble annex typically felt too hot or cold. On that late November day, I felt chilled and still wore my winter coat inside. Our teacher had been interrupted from his lecture for a secretive conversation outside. He returned momentarily, his shoulders sunken, worry crossing his otherwise composed face. President Kennedy has been shot in Dallas; the president's status remains unclear. No... this is not a teaching scheme; this is real and irreconcilable.

No kidding.

As chatter crisscrossed the room, he asked for order. In this American History class, he had much to share about the farsighted men who first filled the nation's highest offices. A young and inspired educator, he wanted us to learn and appreciate and remember. I cannot recall what he told us during those suspenseful minutes following breaking news, but even then, I grasped the irony of an assassination attempt in Dallas while learning about the nation's Founding Fathers, the majesty and nobility of democratic leadership, the eternal values of fairness and freedom they represented.

Before the period ended, someone again summoned our teacher. Juvenile cynicism also left the room. As minutes passed, it seemed that he had abandoned us, and prattle among students raised unanswered questions and uncommon concerns.

Our teacher returned, this time informing us that President Kennedy had been assassinated. His eyes filled with tears as he tried to steady his emotions, a momentous instant because never had I seen any of my teachers display unbridled sadness, especially a man, especially in the early nineteen sixties. That memory haunts me to this day because back then we thought of our teachers as greater than human—strong, resolute, wise—authority figures, duly feared and respected. Tears had no place in a 1963 classroom.

American History ended, and, dazed and bewildered, I trudged to my art class, overseen by a stern matron who shared little of herself. Unlike my American History teacher, this hardened educator did not outwardly embrace the gravity of the day's news, but she did allow a small black-and-white television into her classroom, another major break in protocol. She instructed us to work quietly on our assigned art projects while we listened to unraveling news about a catastrophe in Texas. Try to be creative and stay focused on your art projects, she said.

Following my final class on that gray Friday, I raced home to a weekend dominated by television and waking hours spent absorbing the news along with neighborhood playmates. My emotions skittered from fascination to anger and despondency to excitement. Though barely age fourteen, part of me understood that I was witnessing history firsthand, not just learning about it. I watched in real time as nightclub owner Jack Ruby shot accused assassin Lee Harvey Oswald—the unexpected stun of a pistol blast and raw astonishment washing over nearby cops and journalists—the only time I have witnessed gun violence play out on television in real time, live, uncensored, and unedited.

A long weekend and national day of mourning lingered, and I experienced irreversible loss of a personal hero who had inspired me to think beyond the boundaries of that time and place. His youthfulness, charisma, and active family had become benchmarks for civic engagement, not just theoretical abstractions that we studied in history books.

A national psychodrama unfolded through the fantasy delivery medium of broadcast television—where Saturday morning cartoons, western movies, and charming family sitcoms such as *Father Knows Best* typically filled weekends. But this was an epochal televised experience; this was not make-believe. Kennedy was a great man shot dead while sitting next to his lovely wife dressed gaily in a matching pink dress and pillbox hat.

President John F. Kennedy's death and its aftermath became intractable memories rendered in black and white. His demise darkened who I was then and inexorably adds shading to this present moment, as today's "breaking news" on cable television too frequently showcases radical Islamic terrorism and assassinations of random innocent people.

Is there any other event in human experience that has more potential to change who we are? Death is a permanent loss. There's no room for compromise. No gray areas. It's black and white. Boom. Living or dead. Someone we love or admire dies, and in this life, we will never experience them again other than in memories and memorials.

Character involves traits such as trustworthiness, respectfulness, caring, fairness, and taking responsibility for oneself and the welfare of others. Can death strengthen these positive attributes associated with a person of good character?

With John Kennedy's death, I believe the nation became less trusting. Many things changed on the national stage. Presidents no longer rode through crowds in open convertibles. Security forces around the president became more resolute and cautious. We experienced our vulnerabilities as freedom-loving people when we understood that a single shooter hiding in an upper story window of a book depository could take the life of a president so widely admired, so accessible with his good looks and quick wit. Three shots ring out...boom, boom, boom...dead.

It followed that my generation changed also. Kennedy represented to many of us bright optimism about the future. He had his beautiful wife, Jacqueline, and their two children, Caroline and John Junior, could have been charming characters in a family television program, typical of the family programming of that time, such as *My Three Sons* or *Leave It to Beaver*. It seemed incomprehensible that such a show-business-like family could be assaulted and decimated with an assassin's bullet.

That one day in Dallas destroyed some of our innocence. Though still young and eager, many of us in secondary school became more cynical and less enamored of politically powerful people. The years following Kennedy's assassination, and then the slaying of his brother Bobby and Civil Rights leader Martin Luther King, became a preamble to years of conflict between young and old. The counterculture and voluble opposition to the Vietnam War can in some ways be traced back to November 22, 1963, when our worldview changed by a single, horrible day in Dallas, Texas.

Children and teens of that time did not give up on hope and optimism. To me, it's always been sociologically interesting that the most successful rock 'n' roll band of the twentieth century became part of a national obsession within months after the Kennedy assassination.

The Beatles jumped onto the American stage with a force that pundits have described as the *British Invasion*. These four "Lads from Liverpool" renewed our national youth psyche while becoming a new benchmark for fame and success. It was as if they became the therapeutic ointment to counteract the horror of televised assassination, allowing for some healing. The Beatles were indeed a distraction that the youth of America badly needed because we had been changed and chastened by the fatal vulnerabilities of an American president and his family.

I also changed. Though I was barely a teen, I recall a much more heightened sense of susceptibility, not so much for my existence but for the values that knitted the nation together. How could anybody kill a great American president mainly for his policies about Cuba, so pundits have conjectured through the decades that have followed? What about the beneficent policies he stood for such as the Peace Corps or boldly and safely landing a man on the moon within ten years? Hadn't he made substantial progress around race relations? Didn't he inspire respect from other nations, such as the adoring French who idolized his wife, Jacqueline? Isn't the Secret Service vigilant and armed enough to shelter our president, the embodiment of the principles of our Constitution, our Commander in Chief?

Marian Wright Edelman addressed the perpetuity of unfinished business in the assassination of this admired president: "So much of the deep lingering sadness over President Kennedy's assassination is about the unfinished promise: unspoken speeches, unfulfilled hopes, the wondering about what might have been."[35]

I believe that the children of those times are still processing the personal implications and meaning of John F. Kennedy's assassination, ambiguity they sometimes revisit each reoccurring November 22nd, anniversary of the assassination. The impact of a major event at such a formative time in life cannot be fully articulated, but for those of us now

---

35 Brainyquotes.com: http://www.brainyquote.com/quotes/keywords/assassination.html

twenty and thirty years older than Kennedy was when slain by Oswald, this murder continues to be a yardstick and a lens through which we think about contemporary events and political leaders. Some of what we experienced in our youth has been passed on to our children, whether it is a healthy suspicion of governmental cover-ups or disillusionment with the American myth of being the greatest nation in the history of humanity.

One awful death resonates from the past even today. The post-World War II American character has never since been as trusting or respectful of the institutions of government. We continue to search for new leaders who can consistently inspire optimism, pride, vigor, and resolute determination to make a difference, as did John F. Kennedy. The good news here is that we keep trying; our national character includes a steadfast commitment to creating *a more perfect union.* We shall always seek leaders who might help us achieve our national values, our preferred exceptionalism on the international stage.

Loss does not mean that a person's character will change as an absolute given, nor does it mean that the impact of loss improves character. Psychopaths and sociopaths live among the general population. To some, loss inspires tunnel-vision and revenge. To others, loss encourages self-loathing and deterioration of the spirit. Still others never recover from loss and become stuck, unable to grow or evolve further. They lock the doors and hide away for the rest of their lives.

But it seems that for most of us, loss adds to character by increasing wisdom, appreciation, empathy, and gratitude. Loss makes us more capable of helping children and grandchildren learn and accept all the realities of existence, especially the impermanence of life and thus the value of growth and achievement and progress across the lifespan.

Ronnie Janoff-Bulman, Ph.D., Professor Emeritus of the University of Massachusetts, delineated a remarkable theory about the psychological impact of loss. Her theory begins with the notion that most of us pursue our daily lives governed by three fundamental assumptions: 1) the world is benevolent—we can expect good fortune and outcomes; 2) the world is meaningful—events in our lives correspond to our good or bad behaviors; and, 3) the self is worthy—we have the power to control positive or negative outcomes. These three assumptions serve as a basis for our sense of well-being; they give meaning and stability to our lives. They help us remain optimistic about tomorrow.

Janoff-Bulman's "The Theory of Shattered Assumptions" asserts that loss and trauma shatter these undeclared but implicit assumptions about the world. When something terrible and unexpected happens, our worldviews become shattered with potentially traumatic consequences, especially among those whose lives are generally positive. The most successful and blessed among us can fall hardest when implicit assumptions shatter due to traumatic events. A typical reaction to discordant trauma is to question everything assumed to be normal. Shattered assumptions can impale us, leaving us confused, hopeless, pessimistic, and distrustful of the future.

Dr. Janoff-Bulman believes that coping with and recovering from extreme trauma is possible when we learn to confront, address, and change negative thought patterns occurring after trauma and loss. We can become less conscious of our vulnerability and mortality and reengage in life; we can "go boldly where no one has gone before." After bereavement, there is hope. With support from others who love us as well as deliberate introspection, such as thoughtfully answering some of the questions posed throughout this book, we can mend our shattered lives and move forward.[36]

ISIS

If when seeing the title of this section, your mind immediately conjured up a despicable radical Islamic terrorist sect that has become the world's leading extremist threat, I cannot blame you. Media today regularly

---

36 "The Theory of Shattered Assumptions," as conceived and introduced by Ronnie Janoff-Bulman, Ph.D., and summarized on Wikipedia: https://en.wikipedia.org/wiki/Shattered_Assumptions_Theory

cover the outrage, cruelty, and immorality of one aberrant and dysfunctional slice of an otherwise peaceful religion worshiped by 1.6 billion people worldwide. ISIS today stands for the Islamic State for Iraq and Syria, and those who pledge allegiance show unrelenting intolerance for others who do not agree with their strict and unforgiving interpretations of the Holy Quran.

But *Isis* has always meant something entirely different to me, a soft place in my heart for an animal that represents much of my twenties, a time of youthful potency and buoyant optimism for the future. Isis was a "good girl," a gentle German shepherd owned by my high school friend. She lived much of her life in the Kansas Flint Hills, a farm dog always available for long walks. I spent many weekend days hiking with her while experiencing the simple joys of fresh air and untrammeled tallgrass prairies, the solitude and majesty of wide open spaces.

When I was age 32, Becky and I moved to Colorado Springs, Colorado, for me to begin a new job and career with the area's largest and most successful advertising agency, Gabel Advertising. I moved to Colorado ahead of her by several weeks, and then finally she moved our remaining belongings and joined me in March 1981 in the beautiful city at the foot of Pikes Peak. During our first dinner together following her long drive across Kansas and eastern Colorado, she mentioned in passing that Isis had died a few days earlier, and the news hit me with as much impact as if my best friend had died. All readers who have owned and cared for pets as if "fur children" understand this flood of emotion. Although Isis wasn't technically my dog, she was my hiking buddy who had covered many miles of growth and maturation with me, and I believe she considered me to be something akin to an uncle or perhaps a step-father. I thought of her as a fur step-child.

After I had grieved for a few weeks, I wrote a poem. This elegy characterizes the depth of our relationship, man, and dog, and underscores that humans often bond with their pets at levels of intensity equal to and sometimes greater than our ties with other humans. We love our pets, and we also believe our pets love us, unconditionally. When they leave us after their relatively short lives, we experience yet another kind of loss. To read this poem correctly, please read each column from top to bottom and then left to right:

ISIS

"STAY ...
You
Stay
There, Isis."

Her eyes
Engage
With twinkle
Light,
While gold
Grass
Snaps to
Salute the sun,
Slapping my
Worn denim, as
I back from
Her butter eyes
Not budging;
Rather,
Her eyes stick
Solid
To my
Shrinking body,
And she settles,
Stoic, a
Coyote copy.

"You
Stay
THERE," I
Shout stupidly
At her stare,
So steadfast.

Breezes
Wander
Between
The fields
And us,
Filling

The air with
Snap-Crackle-
Pop,
But she waits
While
Rocks
Rest
Under her chin,
Solid—
As if she knows
I won't wait,
Even as
I twist to
Step ahead
And cross
Miles of
Misery.

Lost, I
Switch back to
Toe and heel,
Watching
Her small
Simple shape,
Alone and
Aware, as I,
Of my
Offense...

And my lips,
Full of hush,
Purse dry
To blow the
Wind,
Sending
Shrill
Whistles
To fight
Flint Hills
And finality.

Yet, from a
Million
Miles away,
Her ears twitch,
And she leaps
At silence
Like a Rabbit—
Whooooshhhh.

Through wheat
And
Stubble
She flashes—
A prairie fire—
And seconds
Slice
Space
So suddenly.

Then, beneath
My boots
She squirms
Whining a
Winsome
Welcome.

We walk,
Side by side,
Like shadows
Merging from
Sunset into
Starlight,
Me and Isis—
A wandering
Shepherd,
Soothing my
Spirit and
Married to
My memories
Forever.

QUESTIONS TO CONSIDER ABOUT CHARACTER CHANGES THAT LOSS CAN BRING

*What is the worst thing that changed about you
when you lost someone important?*

*What is the best thing that changed about you
when you lost that same person?*

*Did you see others around you change because of a
shared loss? Were these good or bad changes?*

Do you admire any historical figures who suffered significant losses and thrived beyond their losses? Who and why?

*If you were to lose the person or pet closest to you now, do you hope to
change your character traits for the better? Which traits and why?*

HAS YOUR SELF-ESTEEM CHANGED?

ONE OF MY losses caused significant soul-searching as I considered how a good friend could die, and I didn't find out about his passing until *nine months* after his death. What kind of friend had I been? Was I unworthy not to know about his rapid illness and death until almost a year after he died? Let me explain.

Every holiday season his greeting card arrived, one of the few handwritten cards we received each year. Most people have discontinued holiday cards altogether or instead they mail form letters filled with glad tidings and exuberant news and photos about children and grandchildren. He always wished us health and success for the new year and usually offered a punchline, some ironic twist on life's everyday absurdities. He promised to stop and see us in Denver during one of his epic road trips. His cars were his children, nurtured, maintained, and nudged to greatness.

The first child I met was a taxicab-yellow Porsche. Behind the wheel, wearing sunglasses, he looked like a leading man: dashing, cocky, alpha. It is anyone's guess how many times that sports car zipped from LA to Colorado and points east, but many. Then he adopted a bright red Miata, providing even less practical luggage space than the Porsche. But he found a creative way to strap his luggage to the Miata's trunk rack, being well equipped and provisioned for weeks on the road. He brushed off my practical concerns that the contents of his luggage may be ruined in rain or snow or end up scattered along an interstate highway.

As the years piled on, he finally became more sensible about his peripatetic nature and proclivity to drive through the mountains of Utah and Colorado. A Jeep Grand Cherokee became his ultimate road-trip-ping metal-child, and he equipped it with technological luxuries: GPS, CB radio, radar detector, and a great music system. Like its pretentious brothers, the Jeep pressed a lot of pavement, so much so that he even replaced the entire engine instead of buying a new car or a newer used car. He found accomplishment in rehabbing and refurbishing rather than replacing. His scrupulous restorations of aging cars always created something better than the originals.

John Christian Miller loved cars in the same way he loved life. He enjoyed the journey as much as any other man I have known, finding reasons to remain confident and excited despite occasional setbacks. He was witty, funny, articulate—blessed with a powerful, resonating, room-filling voice. His quickness attested to the decades that he had spent as a leading LA radio news anchor, growing into AM radio during its heyday, always slightly ahead of his time but in step with the zeitgeist. Equally at ease on television as he pitched the miracle of Ginsu knives or the shrewd investment potential of gold coins, casual in the presence of celebrities, earnest about free enterprise, John Darin, as his stage name portrayed, was as smooth and pleasing as Bobby, the 1950's folk-pop music icon who must have inspired the radio veteran's pseudonym.

John Darin, or JD as I nicknamed him, was a friend apart, a periodic rush of positive energy who would check in by phone or email just to see how we were doing. He usually had a new post-retirement scheme to make money in areas as divergent as pitching affordable pre-need cremation plans to growing non-GMO soybeans in Brazil. He looked to the future as bright with possibilities.

During the holiday season of 2013, his traditional card did not ar-rive. I had been mildly concerned, knowing somewhere in the recesses of my mind that he was a predictable friend I'd known for twenty-four years. He should have been in touch by then. But I had let it go: no flash-ing warning signs. It had taken me almost a year from his last email to become concerned.

When walking around a lake near my home, I dispatched a quick email from my iPhone. It bounced instantly. Could JD have changed internet service providers without letting me know? Not fathomable. Then I called his home office number. Disconnected. I tried his cell phone number. Also, disconnected. I sped-walked home, wondering what had happened.

Becky was the first to discover the truth as revealed by a Google keyword search. Dick Heatherton, a famous radio and television personality and brother of Joey Heatherton, a well-known singer and actress from the sixties and seventies, had written a deeply felt lamentation about John's death.

The digest version goes like this: Severe back pain during the 2013 holiday season had forced JD to seek medical attention, and the diagnosis could not have been more brutal: pancreatic cancer. JD's journey from diagnosis to death didn't last more than ten weeks. He died March 9, 2014. The news spread, but not everywhere.

He had died almost nine months before it occurred to me that I should get in touch and find out when he would be coming to visit Becky and me in Denver. Although his substantial LA radio circle of colleagues and friends knew of his illness and death, I was dumbstruck ignorant. JD's death hit me as a cold slap: the Google query we never want to see.

Could he have called me? Didn't he know that I would have been there in whatever way I could? Did he think of Becky and me during his final weeks of pain and suffering, dulled by narcotics? Not even an email? Did he reach for his cell phone to call then hesitated as another shooting pain overwhelmed his consciousness, or a morphine drip dulled him to senselessness?

This is a different kind of death than I have ever experienced: a dying process that is disconnected from my awareness. In this networked society, where most news travels around the globe on Twitter within seconds, is it possible for a friend to get sick and die and a long-term friend not have a clue until nine months after his death?

All these questions have no answers. The answers have died too. To reconcile this dissonance, I can imagine how it might have been had he called.

(Ring, ring)

"Hello … hey, JD, how the heck have you been!?"

"Well, under the weather to be truthful."

"A cold or flu? I hope you're on the other side of it now."

"Actually, it's more severe." Pregnant pause. *"I have pancreatic cancer."*

"That's horrible news, JD. Have your doctors figured out a treatment plan yet? Newer targeted drugs are showing a lot of promise."

"The plan is to keep me comfortable. That's all they can do. Cancer has already taken over most of my internal organs."

"No surgeries? No chemo?"

"It's too late for that. So… how's Becky? How have you been?"

I understand how horrendous conversations like this might be for someone terminally ill. How difficult it must be to nurture others trying to find words and understand their emotions when death comes knocking. An exuberant man full of life and laughter would not want to close his final days with one downer telephone conversation after another. He was too witty for that. Too ironic and clever.

But I am guilty of complacency about the facts of our brief time on earth. Maybe that's a trick of the mind: to close out the possibility that this day may be my last or only two months remain. Perhaps creating a sense of permanence in an impermanent existence helps mortals move through the days without becoming paralyzed by certain probabilities: disease, death, and disappearance of a too-distant friend.

I keep 95 percent of the non-spam emails I receive. Fortunately, long ago I labeled an Outlook folder "John Darin." During the rush of disbelief and grief after discovering Dick Heatherton's blog tribute to our mutual friend, I returned to that folder to read JD's final email message to me. It came shortly after Thanksgiving in 2013 and just a few weeks before he would receive the shocking news of his imminent death.

He wrote: *Thinking of you guys at holiday time. Long overdue for a Denver visit. Maybe early next year.* He then shared a brief rundown of his travel plans for the holidays: from LA to Seattle, to Chicago, busy and frenetic and, as always, connecting with a wide circle of family and friends. His travel destinations were more about people than places. Then he signed off: *see you again soon maybe, Yewtaw John Darin.* (LA manicured through-and-through, he loved the western aura bestowed by his retirement home in Utah, cowboy boots and all.)

Now I know that "maybe" was significant: hesitation and uncertainty coming from someone always so confident about the future. JD didn't just skim over the possibilities of his days as if a stone skipping the surface of life; he dove into his plans, becoming immersed with gusto.

Maybe mattered then, and I didn't understand.

To this day, I wonder why I did not have the intuitive insights or relationship skills that would have given me an early warning that something was wrong, very wrong with my friend's health.

Loss comes in many forms. We can lose a job, a career, a home, a friend—even a purpose. With loss often comes a harsh blow to self-esteem. It is common to feel deflated and defeated, less worthy than when we were working successfully, paying bills, counting on someone, or having crystal-clarity about our journey forward. Not only do we sometimes struggle with our sense of self-worth, but we may also experience other painful emotions such as depression, anxiety, fear, or futility. Gaining something usually buoys our spirits; losing that something cuts deep, piercing into the foundation of our life.

When we lose someone close and dear, we may have similar feelings. We may feel sad, uptight, pessimistic, or angry. Sometimes we can experience all those troubling feelings cycling in and out of our daily experiences. With loss of a person close to us, we may also feel abandonment and loneliness. Loss is one of life's most difficult challenges, guaranteed to all of us should we live long enough.

FURTHER QUESTIONS ABOUT
LOSS AND SELF-ESTEEM

Has someone close to you passed away, leaving you wondering if you measured up: by supporting him or her enough?

How do you come to terms with the loss of someone close and a lingering possibility that you may have failed to be entirely empathetic about their pain and suffering, and giving of your time and resources?

Have you known someone else who lost a loved one and had unresolved feelings of failure in the relationship? What have you said and done that offered the most comfort?

If you could have a conversation with someone dearly departed, a friend or lover with whom you still have unfinished business, what would you like to say?

What can you do now to restore your self-esteem and move on?

HAVE YOU BEEN BLESSED?
WOULD YOU BLESS OTHERS?

THESE ARE AMONG the most challenging and personal questions to answer. Being blessed as it commonly has been understood involves someone from a church tradition providing a blessing in the form of a prayer or other ritualistic action: a priest, pastor, mullah, or rabbi. The other context in which I understand the notion of a blessing is when something of good fortune happens in life that might be attributed to Divine intervention: God, Jesus Christ, Mohammad, Abraham, or other historical religious figures. We hear people proclaim their blessings with such statements as, "I was blessed with a healthy grandson," or "My wife was blessed to recover from incurable cancer." Blessings come from either ritualistic action by religious ceremony practitioners or by happenstance from supernatural or Divine intervention: miracles that cannot easily be explained without evocation of a deity.

Instead of exploring religious orthodoxy about the nature of blessings, I would rather examine blessings from an existential perspective: how we choose to acknowledge and appreciate the good things that happen to us and how we support others with selfless and even anonymous acts of kindness. In either case, these are actions within our control rather than dependent on actions by others, whether a pastor's blessing or God's apparent intervention in our lives.

Have I been blessed? Most of us might begin to answer this question with a quick survey of our life history. For example, I survived severe asthma attacks in childhood that nearly took my life. So, I was blessed then to survive. I can recall several occasions when, in retrospect, my risky behavior could have led to my death, such as driving a car under the influence of alcohol as a teen. It became a blessing that my risky behavior did not end in a fatal accident. That was a blessing indeed.

But I can also consider this question through the lens of criticism. Have I had any of the "big breaks" that some celebrities report experiencing at the beginning of their careers? Someone meets someone by accident. Someone is working at McDonald's, and a movie mogul takes notice of a sparkling personality or a look that foreshadows a celebrity-in-the-making. Or somehow a screenplay comes to the attention of a Hollywood director who takes on the project and makes the unknown writer famous and fruitful, seemingly overnight. Or a garage band's gig at a local bar includes in the audience one patron who is an emissary from one of the big record labels. That's how the supergroup *Kansas* became an "overnight sensation."

For example, consider Andy Weir, author of *The Martian*, a bestselling novel that inspired a screenplay that became a 2015 "Best Picture" nominee for the Academy Awards. The backstory goes like this: Andy could not find a traditional publisher to consider his book; thus, the unknown bard self-published using Amazon's CreateSpace platform. He sold the book as a Kindle download for $.99, the lowest allowable price. He gave away chapters on his personal website to build an organic fan base. His book's success began fitfully with persistent self-promotion among a small but expanding group of online fans. Eventually, his Kindle book soared into the ranks of digital bestsellers. Then Broadway Books, an imprint of the Crown Publishing Group, noticed the growing buzz around Andy's book. The publisher offered him a traditional publishing agreement, and more than 28,500 Amazon reader reviews later, averaging 4.6 out of 5 stars, Weir's book achieved sales ranking among the Top 100 books, hitting the #2 spot. Someone in film development noticed the success of his book and brought the story to the attention of Ridley Scott, one of Hollywood's most vaunted and successful directors.

Yes, the same Ridley Scott who directed many acclaimed blockbuster movies such as *Alien, Blade Runner, Thelma & Louise,* and *Gladiator.*

Was Andy Weir blessed? Did he win the "blessings lottery"? This is a question with no definitive answer, but sometimes it is hard to explain why the "fickle finger of fate" chooses some artists over others. Weir worked hard to achieve these breakthroughs as a writer and book self-promoter, but maybe we can agree that other talented and hard-working writers are not so blessed and never become discovered by Hollywood. Over 30,000 books get published every year, and perhaps we can agree that among all those titles are a handful of other books as deserving for big publishing contracts and Hollywood adaptations.

Consider Vincent van Gogh as another example, who lived just 37 years and left the world with almost two thousand works of art. All his masterpieces were underappreciated during his fleeting existence. He only sold one painting during his entire life; fortunately, his generous brother, Theo, supported this penniless artist. Van Gogh died impover-ished in 1890 by suicide. He has been quoted presciently lamenting, "I can't change the fact that my paintings don't sell. But the time will come when people will recognize that they are worth more than the value of the paints used in the picture."[37] And, indeed, that prediction became more than true, well beyond the artist's wildest dreams of future com-mercial success. He is now considered a master with an incalculable im-pact on art and culture. *Portrait of Dr. Gachet,* van Gogh's study of a medic who cared for him during the final months of his life, broke records when the painting sold in 1990 for $152 million.

Was Vincent van Gogh blessed?

I can honestly attest to my belief that I have not been "blessed" in the sense of being discovered by someone who instantly changes the direc-tion of my life and fortunes. That's a dream shared by most artists, but only a handful can probably claim such blessings.

---

37 van Gogh, Vincent, as quoted on awesomestories.com: https://www.awesomesto-ries.com/asset/view/Vincent-Van-Gogh

Again, I can step back and look at my life and indeed find many blessings. I was born in the right country, to the right parents, at the right time in history. I have lived comfortably, never facing the agonies of poverty or homelessness. I have had the freedoms that come with running my company, spending much of my career as my boss. Becky and I have had a few interesting opportunities to travel overseas and explore the wider world. And as a writer, I have had some impact on thinking about Baby Boomers, aging, and business. I have never achieved fame or stardom, but I have had opportunities to influence others through my writing and speaking. So, from an aerial view of my life, I have been blessed. Amazing things have not happened, but neither have truly horrible things.

This leads me to a conclusion: deciding whether I have been blessed is my choice to agree with or not agree, rather than a state of being that can be universally defined, then declared or denied. Almost everyone reading these words must attest to blessings in their life when comparing their life to the millions of homeless and hungry throughout the world. Even those of us who feel that real miracles have not occurred in our lives must admit that feeling blessed is easy when considering how lousy life has been and can be for billions of deceased and living humans. Just reflecting upon the potential cruelties and injustices of life should nudge most of us into a state of greater gratitude.

We can assume the role of a passive wannabe when answering the question, "Have I been blessed?" Or we can conclude that feeling blessed is a decision based upon perception and perspective. So, in the context of all human history and the 7.43 billion humans living today, most of us have been blessed with the basics of comfortable living, way beyond a subsistence level, as well as opportunities to "shoot for the stars."

Thus, I arrive at this answer: "Yes, I have been blessed, very blessed."

The second question is more a matter of choice and volition: "Would you bless others?" The question isn't "Do you bless others?" but rather, "Would you?" That's where an answer can become more daunting. "Under what circumstances would I bless others?" "All?" "Some?"

"None?" The greatest, most compassionate humans that history remembers tend to fall into the category of "All." Think of Mother Theresa or Mahatma Gandhi as examples. These were extraordinary people who sacrificed much and lived in constant service to others. They would bless others by their daily actions and choices. From my reading about these exceptional humans, they would not compromise when it came to blessing others through practical action, such as feeding the poor or accepting incarceration instead of giving up principles of nonviolent civil disobedience.

My truthful answer to this question so far in my journey must be: "I would bless some others under certain circumstances but not in other situations." My agreement to bless others is inherently conditional, and that is a source of sadness to me even as I try to become more accepting of others, more giving, less self-centered or materialistic.

When I was a graduate student in psychology, the reigning therapeutic approach my professors advocated and taught was a process developed by the late Carl Rogers. He was a famous "humanistic psychologist" who promoted the concept of "unconditional positive regard," which simply means embracing necessary acceptance and support of a person regardless of what that person says or does. This level of empathy and acceptance of someone else creates optimum conditions for a patient to gain psychological insights and learn to accept personal responsibility for feelings, thoughts, and actions. Called *client-centered therapy*, this approach to helping others with emotional difficulties means that the therapist learns to set aside her beliefs, opinions, and biases to fully accept the other. In one sense, unconditional positive regard is a way of bestowing someone with a tangible and potentially life-changing blessing.

Rogers once explained the basic premise and therapeutic potential of unconditional positive regard from his experiences:

For me, it expresses the primary theme of my whole professional life, as that theme has been clarified through experience, interaction with others, and research. This theme has been utilized and found effective in many different areas, until the broad label "a person-centered approach" seems the most descriptive. The central hypothesis of this approach can be briefly stated. It is that the individual has within him or herself vast resources for self-understanding, for altering her or his self-concept, attitudes, and self-directed behavior—and that these resources can be tapped if only a definable climate of facilitative psychological attitudes can be provided.[38]

In a word, a "definable climate of facilitative psychological attitudes" can be thought of as simply bestowing a *blessing* on someone else. Just as a Rogerian psychotherapist can create an atmosphere of acceptance and empathy, we also have a choice to live more in a state of *becoming* a blessing to others. To me, this means emotional movement from concern for my welfare and achievements toward a passion for the well-being and achievements of others. I think most of us agree that we can and sometimes do step outside ourselves and realize a real sense of empathy for the plights and challenges being experienced by others. We accept others despite their foibles, hang-ups, and destructive behaviors. We offer helping hands when we can. We donate time and money for less fortunate. But my experience has been that most of us fall short of the ideal. We get caught up in the messiness and uncertainties in our lives and thus sometimes ignore how we can be a transformative blessing to others. We become self-centered rather than client-centered. Carl Rogers believed we all have within us the resources for personal growth, the innate capability to achieve a state of grace; we can choose to become more of a blessing to others, making progress, not necessarily achieving perfection.

Religious leaders, spiritual teachers, and character guides through the millennia have encouraged their followers to try and assume a

---

38 Rogers, Carl R. "Client-centered Approach to Therapy," in I. L. Kutash and A. Wolf (eds.), *Psychotherapist's Casebook: Theory and Technique in Practice.* San Francisco: Jossey-Bass

mental framework of acknowledging our blessings and then blessing others. We all have tough days and unfortunate experiences, and sometimes, as my wise father counseled, we fail to "smell the roses." It can be so powerful to shift our mental framework, to see clearer skies where we may have only seen dark clouds hanging over our lives. This positive context does not necessarily mean we must deny reality, eschewing the negative forces, personalities, and circumstances in our lives. Legions of teachers and coaches have taught that we do indeed have the power to shift the framework of how we interpret the meaning of what happens to us. Still, other teachers have counseled that we will find our blessings by only acting in ways that bless others: being a strong shoulder when needed, helping those less fortunate through philanthropy, and being an outspoken advocate for values that contribute to rather than subtract from the lives of others.

Maya Angelou, widely recognized as "America's Poet Laureate," understood the unique power of charity by being a blessing to others: "The thing to do, it seems, is to prepare yourself so you can be a rainbow in somebody else's cloud. Somebody who may not look like you. May not call God the same name you call God—if they call God at all. I may not dance your dances or speak your language. But be a blessing to somebody. That's what I think."[39]

39 Angelou, Maya, "Be a Rainbow in Someone Else's Cloud," as recorded in video and available on YouTube: https://www.youtube.com/watch?v=wtdffxj7pNE

OTHER QUESTIONS ABOUT OUR BLESSINGS

What stands out in your life as your most cherished blessings? Did you have any control over these blessings?

How might you change your perspective about blessings so that you feel more blessed more often?

Can you transform a destructive relationship in your life by blessing a person who is causing you to suffer?

Thinking about historical figures, who is your benchmark for their selflessness and willingness to live as a blessing to others?

What might you change about yourself, whether attitudes or behaviors or both, that will help you become more of a blessing to others?

IS THERE POWER IN THE USE OF MERCY?

AN ONLINE SEARCH for the meaning of the word mercy returns the following denotation: *compassion or forgiveness shown toward someone whom it is within one's power to punish or harm.* This definition implies adopting a tenderhearted mental state in reaction to being injured by someone, showing compassion or forgiveness when our raw instincts may be to lash out and punish. This definition implies an even more strenuous test: acting on feelings of compassion or forgiveness by doing something proactive such as stopping a punishment, giving the injurer financial or material aid, or providing positive testimony to others about the character and worthiness of the injurer. Acting—doing something positive for someone who injures us—requires another level of commitment to mercy, implying additional cost or inconvenience above and beyond the mental act of merely feeling compassionate or forgiving.

I recall a very early lesson in compassion that has provided me with a benchmark for this sense of charity toward others. Although this anecdote could seem rather trivial in an adult context, the lesson was nevertheless meaningful to me as it amplified the power of mercy over condemnation and exclusion. My actions pointed the way to grace, both as a mental state and a process involving positive actions.

David was a popular kid in elementary school, brilliant and precocious. He was gregarious and a leader on the playground, and for whatever reasons, he teased me incessantly. (I've always been easy to tease!) He was the kind of kid who always had some smartass comeback or veiled criticism. I liked him for his sense of humor and quick wit, but, of course, I was sometimes hurt by his incisive criticisms, veiled as they were through bombast and innuendo. I wanted to earn his positive regard for me, but my attempts were always frustrated for inexplicable reasons. He wouldn't get off my back, and I resented him for it, which meant I usually tried to avoid him.

I was a creative kid and one time became fascinated with the idea of hosting and staging a Halloween party. I planned this experience to be much more than the typical costume affair. Having at that time been sufficiently frightened and inspired by late-night shock TV movies about Frankenstein and Dracula, I planned a party that would include all kinds of scary interactive experiences. For example, when blindfolded, my guests would be dared to hold yucky organs in their hands. Cooked warm spaghetti became rat intestines and peeled grapes became cat eyeballs. Cow bones became human bones. I created other unexpected audio and visual surprises in my basement to terrify, delight, and inspire my young guests.

At school, a few weeks before October 31st, I gave my preferred guests creative party invitations, and my enthusiasm for this event became captivating among my peers. I intentionally did not give David an invitation. Withholding an invitation was my juvenile way of withholding mercy as punishment for all his teasing. News of my party continued to spread among my peers, and soon the party became quite an event, much anticipated and discussed on the recess playground.

David was cagey not to confront me about not inviting him, but every time I ran into him he would smile brightly and proclaim, "Happy Halloween!" At first, his brash pronouncements embarrassed me because he was so bold and apparently nonplussed about being uninvited. But as the cheerful greetings continued, encounter after encounter, I began to feel guilty for not inviting him. I recall having a very ambiguous debate with myself about the pros and cons of including David on my guest list. I may have asked my parents what they thought would be the right thing to do in this situation. I did not want David at my party if he would use the confab as another occasion to keep teasing and putting me down, perhaps embarrassing me further in front of our peers. In more of an adult context, I did not want David to take away my power as creator and host of the party. This party was going to be my opportunity to demonstrate my creativity and impress peers. Alternatively, I could empathize with how he might feel about being excluded from a party that all our peers were discussing and anticipating. Sometimes feeling as if an underdog, I could step into his probable feelings about being left out and how horrible it was as a young person to be ostracized from a peer group.

Most of us grow up confronting similar situations. We have experienced circumstances when others fail to communicate honestly with us, and this becomes a form of ostracism that can be devastating. No matter what we do to make amends or clear the air, those alienating others continue to treat us unmercifully—emotionally and psychologically pushing us aside. This leads to social alienation, as defined by Jan Hajda, a sociology theorist:

> Alienation is an individual's feeling of uneasiness or discomfort which reflects his exclusion or self-exclusion from social and cultural participation. It is an expression of nonbelonging or non-sharing, an uneasy awareness or perception of unwelcome contrast with others. It varies in its scope and intensity. It may be restricted to a few limited situations, such as participation in a peer group, or it may encompass a wide social universe, including participation in the larger society.[40]

One of the profound insights I learned during my undergraduate education came to me through a scholarly journal article written by one of my favorite college professors: "Social Alienation by Communication Denial," by Dr. Kim Giffin, published in *The Quarterly Journal of Speech*. I have saved a copy of the good professor's article for all these years. Dr.

---

40 Hajda, Jan, "Alienation and Integration of Student Intellectuals," American Sociological Review, XXXVI, (October 1961), 758-759

Giffin perceptively observed that when we are denied reliable communication with someone else, the typical reaction is to withdraw, sometimes with destructive consequences; we may become unmerciful in our responses.

> Withdrawal behavior in response to communication denial involves acceptance of the implication of the denial—that one is somehow unworthy of communication with a certain person or persons. Acceptance of this implication is much more common than many people believe. It is not at all uncommon for a person to believe he is unworthy of talking to people with more influence, more education, more experience, or just more self-assurance. Without acceptance of this somewhat preposterous notion, withdrawal from interaction and the resultant high degree of social alienation could not take place.[41]

Finally, after several days of deliberation, I gave David a formal invitation. He was genuinely pleased and grateful and became quite empathetic toward me in return. His criticisms became compliments. At the party, he was one of the most enthusiastic guests, adding to the theatrics by playing along with my tricks and party surprises. In turn, I felt liberated from someone who seemed always to be my critic through cynicism and innuendo and dismissals. He never teased me again other than through harmless banter typical of most friendly relationships between boys. Maybe he came to respect me because he recognized that I demonstrated compassion by inviting him to my party when I could have socially ostracized him. It had been in my power to punish by exclusion, and I had instead chosen forgiveness and inclusion. My reward was liberation from complicated, harsh feelings I had felt about David: my anger over being the target of his incessant teasing and embarrassment that I did not measure up to his standards of respect-worthiness.

---

41 Giffin, Kim, "Social Alienation by Communication Denial," The Quarterly Journal of Speech, Spring 1972

Rick Warren is a famous Christian pastor, author, and founder and senior pastor of Saddleback Church, an evangelical megachurch in Lake Forest, California, the eighth-largest church in the United States. Warren wrote a short essay on his personal blog, entitled "Don't Be Reluctant to Show Mercy." This adds a more theological perspective:

We all need mercy because we all stumble and fall and require help to get back on track. We need to offer mercy to each other and be willing to receive it from each other

You can't have fellowship without forgiveness because bitterness and resentment always destroy fellowship. Sometimes we hurt each other intentionally and sometimes unintentionally, but either way, it takes massive amounts of mercy and grace to create and maintain fellowship.

The Bible says, 'You must make allowance for each other's faults and forgive the person who offends you. Remember, the Lord forgave you, so you must forgive others.' (Colossians 3:13 NLT).

The mercy God shows to us is the motivation for us to show mercy to others. Whenever someone hurts you, you have a choice to make:

Will I use my energy and emotions for retaliation or resolution?

You can't do both.

Many people are reluctant to show mercy because they don't understand the difference between trust and forgiveness. Forgiveness is letting go of the past. Trust has to do with future behavior.

Forgiveness must be immediate, whether or not a person asks for it. Trust must be rebuilt over time.

Trust requires a track record. If someone hurts you repeatedly, you are commanded by God to forgive them instantly, but you are not expected to trust them immediately, and you are not expected to continue allowing them to hurt you. They must prove they have changed over time."[42]

When unexpected death comes calling, the challenge to achieve a state of mercy becomes much more thought-provoking than my juvenile experiences with David. How common is it for us to feel less than merciful after losing someone we dearly love? When a loved one dies, especially tragically, it is not uncommon to feel vengeful as if abandoned by God. Our reasoning may seem sensible. "If God understood how much I love and need my child, He would not have taken her from us. He would have been merciful and spared her life." Those who believe in the benevolence and love of their creator can sometimes react to tragic loss as if they've been cheated or denied. These are among the most challenging moments in life: accepting an enormous loss with merciful feelings, even for God.

Showing mercy in a theological sense means having forgiveness for God whose plans for us we cannot understand. We may be deeply challenged to forgive or show compassion for God: He did not prevent the accident or illness leading to a child's death, so we conjecture in our most agonizing moments of grief. We may stop going to church or abandon our religious faith altogether. Where can there be power in feeling merciful for the One who stands for mercy?

Based on my review of many stories about humans showing mercy to other humans, the power of mercy displaces negative emotions that can destroy the well-being of the injured. Using compassion as a tool for coping with tragedy can free the injured person from hatred, resentment, hostility, and a sense of powerlessness. Mercy replaces self-destructive emotions that can elicit damaging behaviors such as violence toward the individual who has injured us or those associated with the injurer, or self-destructive injuries such as alcohol and drug abuse. Mercy can be

---

42 Warren, Rick, "Don't Be Reluctant to Show Mercy," as posted on a blog, *Pastor Rick's Daily Hope*, May 21, 2014: https://goo.gl/xbsqyl

spiritually uplifting even if we perceive the injurer to be God because He did not prevent the damage with His infinite powers.

Each of us is likely to confront at some point in our lives the choice to be merciful or not. We may be merciful in thoughts or actions or both. The objective of our mercy may be a living person or not. We may have the opportunity to be merciful in our thoughts when betrayed by friends, lovers, employers, or business associates. We may direct our tender feelings to the source of our spiritual faith. But mercy is power when it liberates us to continue living in a state of acceptance, peace, and hopefulness for the future. "Nothing can make injustice just but mercy," wrote poet Robert Frost.[43]

---

43 Frost, Robert, Brainyquotes.com: Read more at: https://goo.gl/1B0ejN

QUESTIONS CONCERNING THE POWER OF MERCY

What is your most vivid memory of being merciful when you could have instead punished?

When you've been merciful, how has your sense of personal power changed?

Which historical story about mercy is most meaningful to you?

When you have punished someone in the past, how could the outcome and consequences have been improved through mercy?

In a competitive, zero-sum game business world, is mercy old-fashioned and potentially self-defeating?

WHAT CAN ANCESTRAL GENERATIONS TEACH US ABOUT LIVING AND DYING?

MUCH WAS WRITTEN and spoken about the 100th birthday of President Ronald Reagan, on February 6, 2011. This anniversary became a time for many to reflect, to think about this president's legacies and enduring values, a revered elder statesman of the Republican Party. Although my father was a firebrand populist Democrat who sometimes harbored untethered hostility toward President Reagan's economic and social policies, Dad ironically shared some of Reagan's core beliefs, including a love of country and unflinching respect for the principles upon which our nation has been founded: the importance of individual initiative and personal responsibility. On February 20, 2011, my late father would also have celebrated his 100th birthday, just two weeks after Ronald Reagan's. We are losing members of The Greatest Generation at the rate, so this is an important time to pause and consider their sacrifices, accomplishments, and lessons.

MY FATHER'S LESSONS

The autumnal prairie was where I began to understand him: vast, open spaces and dry wind cascading through tall grasses and flint hills; railroad tracks piercing sunset, taking him forever away to where he wanted to be; the stoic determination of hardened, heartland people, meticulously vulnerable.

My father.

While walking among grave markers in a cemetery near my home, Dad kept leaning over my shoulder to remind me of his coaching. He asked me to reflect upon his thundering lectures that I had mistakenly interpreted in childhood as nothing more than corrections.

He told me to consider the superiority of dreams and invention over-accumulation and wealth. Or gently he nudged me to deepen my perspective of moral rectitude supplanting self-serving gain—the victory in not compromising, that power of duty.

Lastly, he required me to grasp the ultimate confrontation with mortality and to possess for myself his stubborn unwillingness to live passively when all the active living had been done ... better not to live at all. Let me go, he said.

My lessons.

There can rarely be completion when a man's father dies. The irre-solvable conflicts. The lingering unworthiness. The profound gratitude. The ephemeral laughter. These notions survive.

His name was Gilbert Green, a taut, bronzed man with twinkling sky-blue eyes, born in the high plains of western Kansas. He had only one brother who was eighteen months older. The Green brothers were an indomitable team, working their chores and fighting their bullies during an unsympathetic time to grow up, of world wars and economic depression.

He fought his battles well, first during World War II in the South Pacific as a cryptographic technician—a Japanese code breaker—and then later as a career employee for the Federal Housing Administration.

One indelible lesson passed from him to me was intolerance of po-litical gamesmanship and unethical decision-making that often follows. I can see him now, red-faced and lit up, pacing the length of his living room, fury spewing over manipulation of laws to serve bureaucrats and money lenders rather than taxpayers.

At the sunset of his career, he endured relentless political pressure re-quiring the FHA to lower its standards for qualifying home loans while accepting the abomination of adjustable-rate mortgages. Dad correctly predicted the eventual outcome more than two decades ahead of schedule. He foresaw that loosening loan restrictions and predatory lending could eventually lead to something akin to the subprime mortgage crisis that contributed to the severe U.S. recession from December 2007 through June 2009.

Work for yourself, he would caution me. Self-employment would be his lifelong dream—to launch a real estate company with his family helping him build an empire. Instead, he punched the federal civil service time-clock for thirty-five years, waking some days with resignation to finish what he had started. He had chosen his path during a time of deprivation; the correct answer always was an unwavering duty to choices.

I remember one day when he took me aside to tell me about a get-rich scheme. It was a period of quickening Baby Boomer fads, with a succession of smash hit products sweeping the nation, from Hula-Hoops to Silly Putty. In our garage, he spoke guardedly to me about a popular toy from his childhood that had been lost to history. He then showed me an old wooden top with a metal tip that he had dug out of a forgotten trunk. By wrapping a string just so around the top and then flinging it with exacting wrist action, he could make the top dance with ferocity. Dad saw it as the next big Boomer craze.

Born with the grit and vision of an entrepreneur, he nevertheless did not also have the willingness to take significant financial risks with limited financial holdings. Bringing his spinning top to market would have required considerable venture capital. At odds with the complexities of national new-product marketing, he eventually let the dream whither.

Dad's after-retirement dreams were of great escapes, where he and my mother might board a silver recreational vehicle and roll into sunset. He wanted nothing fancy or luxurious for himself, just peace of an open road and adventure of another turn. My chronically ill mother dissuaded bold expeditions with her delicate health. He resigned himself instead to fish for bass and crappie in Shawnee Lake, floating above his dreams in a silver rowboat.

Smell the roses, son, he often insisted, as he watched me pushing rashly through the years, head pressed to the proverbial grindstone. He had a clear understanding of mortality, the brevity of our days, and even more elusively, those fleeting moments of joy. I always thought this to be an ironic caution from a man who answered the irritating shout of obligation more frequently than the alluring whisper of possibility.

The years passed with him spending many hours in front of the television. Routine had its predictable, tranquilizing effect, but deep within remained lingering unsatisfied fervor. Every spring he marched into the Kansas state legislature where he fought to protect retired federal employees and their civil service pensions from political capriciousness. In those times when his quick reason and fiery arguments filleted elected thieves, he was never more alive.

As a son searches through the years with only remaining memories to mine, he often uncovers golden nuggets left behind from the man who gave him life. Decades of discussion, telephone calls, and fatherly advice reduce to a few simple aphorisms or an overworked cliché.

Laugh and the world laughs with you; cry and you cry alone, he advised. This was his lesson of perseverance, always remembering that an optimistic outlook and enthusiastic smile can change the day, and on some days, change the world.

His health failed for several years, the inexorable spiral from independence to assisted living, from hospitals to a nursing home. A mild heart attack one morning was all he needed to let go of the reins, and in four difficult months, he passed through the final stages of dependency. After five days of labored breathing, he released his last breath as a gasp and then a resigned sigh.

Gilbert Green now marches decisively through prairie fields, an infinite sea of swaying tall-grass, a 16-guage shotgun snugly under his left arm. Perhaps Uncle Gary is within reach of his shrill whistle should he stumble upon a covey of quail or launch a prairie chicken into frenetic flight. He strides briskly, a bounce in each step. He is in control of this forever moment—no strings attached to lesser bosses or circumstances that prohibited him from achieving some of his dreams. Perhaps parked in the background sits a rolling silver hotel under my mother's control, simple but comfortable. He sees the world as he did during life: for what it gives rather than what it takes.

This, I finally understand.

SAVING US: TRIBUTE TO A DEPARTING GENERATION

In my basement, tucked behind boxes of camping gear, sits a drab olive container about the size of a shoebox. My father once packed it with shotgun shells, and I recall peering over his shoulder decades ago and ogling the bright red and yellow plastic tubes, full of black powder, full of authority, full of power.

As he was moving into assisted-living many years ago, he gave it to me: a practical container, but more importantly, a metaphor. It is a World War II ammo box, an indelible remnant of a war I barely understand, nor have cared much about except as movie entertainment.

But a generation is dying, thousands every month. Newspaper obituary pages have become dotted daily with understated eulogies to these men and women; they are departing quietly in their nineties, with a handful even aging beyond 100.

The demise of this generation is everyday mortality, and yet, leaving with them is a society that once confronted the most difficult choices of freedom and survival. They fought and won the Second Great War; 405,399 Americans made the ultimate sacrifice. Remaining survivors, now becoming feeble with age, are passing with little notice, many warehoused in nursing homes. I ponder if our frenetic society has become too self-absorbed to understand the implications.

For eight decades, the Greatest Generation was our nation's moral compass. Younger generations cannot rival their collective patriotism, sacrifices, or passion for democratic principles. Too few of us have grasped the price they paid for today's prosperity and superpower status.

In *Saving Private Ryan*, Steven Spielberg's movie about the June 1944 invasion of Normandy, France, Captain John Miller said to his reluctant squad member, "When was the last time you felt good about anything?"

How resonant. "Capt. Miller," I answer, "I haven't felt good about the ethical drift of our country for a long time."

We are without an anchor and a generation that has delivered the privileges we take for granted would be correct to feel dismayed: their legacy may soon be forgotten. They are rapidly becoming an *ancestral generation.*

Our present path has become cluttered with entertainment and toys. Self-aggrandizement supersedes self-sacrifice. Selfies trump public service. Inane television sitcoms substitute for family story-telling. Road rage along interstate corridors rivals righteous indignation. Patriotism has been confused with flag waving, and some of those "America: love it or leave it" types would constrain freedom in the name of liberty.

I saw a carbon copy of my father's ammunition box appear as a prop in the Spielberg movie. I thought about Dad and his too-private sacrifices, never discussed as has been the custom of his generation. I saw him and this quiet collection of elderly men and women leaving behind an incomprehensible bushwhack through the twentieth century. I imagined all these old people plodding toward the fading light of sunset and an unceremonious disappearance over the horizon.

If only we could find some way to thank them properly—perhaps carry their values and collective strength forward in this new millennium, inspired by their true ideals.

QUESTIONS ABOUT LIFE AND DEATH
TO ASK OF PAST GENERATIONS

If you could spend one day with a grandparent who has passed away, what questions would you ask about their life and death?

Which of your grandparents died with the greatest dignity and why did this passing impress you?

If you could speak with a coherent Ronald Reagan, free from Alzheimer's disease, what topics would you like to discuss with the former president?

Did you learn valuable lessons about life and living from one of your parents? Which lessons are most enduring and why?

Do you plan to see your departed relatives again, and do you expect to pick up with them where you left off?

WHAT WILL YOU SHARE IN YOUR LAST LECTURE?

———— ⌒⌒ ————

THE SAD NEWS finally arrived in July 2008. Millions had been watching and waiting. Professor Randy Pausch succumbed to the ravages of pancreatic cancer after a noble fight and a noteworthy battle to make the world aware of the disease that killed him. As he wisely observed, pancreatic cancer does not have a celebrity spokesperson because its victims do not live long enough. So, during the final ten months of his life in 2007 and 2008, he had become an accidental national celebrity for an engaging "last lecture" and as an intrepid crusader to fight this disease, even though his demise was inevitable.

Dr. Pausch finished his career as Professor of Computer Science, Human-Computer Interaction and Design at Carnegie Mellon University. He was diagnosed with pancreatic cancer in August 2006, and he undertook aggressive chemotherapies and radiation treatments, but a year later his cancer had metastasized to his liver and spleen. According to his doctors then, he had merely three to six months of functional health remaining.

Carnegie Mellon, as well as some other universities, has a tradition called "The Last Lecture." The context is simple but inspiring: What if you have but one last chance to share your experiences and wisdom with others in the form of a lecture? What enduring values, lessons and ideas would you communicate if this is your final chance?

Professor Pausch, who I will refer to as Randy, gave his last lecture in September 2007, but of course, it was not a hypothetical lecture framework in his case. It was reality; he was dying. But the lecture recorded that day is not about dying; it is about achieving childhood dreams. Randy presented his lecture with enthusiasm, humor, humility, and clarity.

A video recording of this lecture ended up on YouTube, and millions have watched it (approaching 19 million as of this writing). Randy appeared on Oprah's daytime television show and gave a condensed version of the lecture. Jeffrey Zaslow, a journalist with *The Wall Street Journal*, who had attended the live lecture, worked with Randy to write and publish a small book of wisdom and motivational encouragement, entitled *The Last Lecture*. The book topped bestseller lists for weeks following its release in April 2008.

Defying the odds against him, Randy nevertheless lived long enough to see his lecture become a worldwide phenomenon, to watch his book soar to heights of publishing success, to appear on ABC network in an hour-long special with Diane Sawyer, to appear on The Oprah Winfrey Show with eleven precious minutes to communicate his powerful messages, to testify before Congress about the need for research into preventing and curing this horrific disease, to fulfill one of his dreams through a cameo acting role in J. J. Abrams' 2009 cinematic release of *Star Trek*, to give an address in May 2008 for the Carnegie Mellon graduating class, and, finally, to keep his growing list of admirers informed about his journey through a personal website and blog.

Randy wasn't just a dedicated professor, a father of three small children, a husband very much in love with his wife, Jai, and a valiant crusader for those afflicted by fatal diseases. At 47, he was also a young Boomer man who gave members of his generational cohort a glimpse of how an optimistic generation may tackle the final challenges of mortality and eventual dying.

Through his brave journey, he demonstrated the many ways that this next generation of aging mortals will confront the inevitable: by communicating new narratives about the value of human life, by showing how one's final months can be dedicated to sharing timeless wisdom with children and young people, and by *not* going quietly into that dark night.

Randy spent his last days under hospice care, a charitable organization that gives the truest context for reconciliation, remembrance, communication, acceptance, and dignity.

When pondering how the Baby Boomer generation will change dying in the most constructive ways, I realized that those Boomers who address the challenges of a slow dying process would likely choose to die the way they've lived: idealistically, intensely and intently focused on creating a legacy for those who survive. Some will follow in Randy's footsteps. They will give new meaning to the end of our mortal journeys, leaving behind a wiser nation.

Maybe they will help our fragile species finally understand and accept that human life is precious and each person, given the proper context, can contribute meaningfully to our collective journey, even during the final days of life.

Soon after *The Last Lecture* book became available on Amazon.com, I wrote a review that has stood the test of time and still ranks 3rd out of over 2,680 Amazon reviews, garnering 265 out of 304 helpful votes from other readers. My review did stir up some controversy, which both surprised and angered me, but I find the debate to be germane and therefore of value to this discussion. First, here is my book review:

A BIG GIFT OF AFFIRMATION IN A SMALL PACKAGE

As I opened the shipping box from Amazon.com, I found two preordered copies of Randy Pausch's book, one for my family and one for whomever needs it most within the next few weeks. This gift could be for a friend or business acquaintance who has reached some personal crisis or turning point. I'll know. Randy's message will find the right recipient.

This book is an enormous gift in its compact, neatly bound actuality. It is a gift of hope and affirmation, a gift of encouragement and courage.

Recently I said goodbye to a friend and business colleague who at 58 died of pancreatic cancer. His was a more private passing, but nevertheless, he fought the disease until the disease won, and he died with dignity. Two days before his death, he called a mutual friend to wish this friend good luck with a minor corrective surgery. Even two days before death, my stricken friend was thinking of others' welfare. As I sat in his memorial service with 300 other mourners, watching a slide presentation of his photographs and original art, I also thought about Randy Pausch. The two personalities mixed in my mind because they shared so many of the same qualities: creativity, professionalism, gusto for living, a sense of humor, lifelong dedication to giving back to their communities, and a profound faith in personal power.

This is the story of *The Last Lecture*: that we can face any challenge in this life if we welcome our fate with optimism and determination to confront all odds. We can live for the welfare of others. We can live today with our legacies in mind for the future—after we are also gone.

The good professor is his metaphor. In this final gift, he both teaches and does.

Much will be said about this book and its immediate iconic impact on a nation experiencing the doldrums of war, economic turmoil, and loss of standing among other countries. Here is the story of one American sharing the wisdom of our universal humanity, our fragility, our mortality, and our capacities to transcend. Here's one of our best and brightest.

In the ways of passionate storytellers, Randy Pausch and coauthor Jeffry Zaslow tell us how to achieve the most vital of all human yearnings: the realization of childhood dreams. And for adults who believe their dreams have passed them by, this book offers an intuitive methodology to reignite the fires of youthful optimism and fervor.

Within this book's narrative are timeless lessons of showing gratitude, setting goals, keeping commitments, tolerating frustration, maintaining a sense of humor in the face of adversity, telling the truth, working hard, celebrating victories when they arrive, and choosing to be a fun-loving Tigger over a sad-sack Eeyore.

Life is short, a fact affirmed once again with the passing of Randy Pausch on July 25, 2008. This "last lecture" is no less significant for the young and healthy as it is for the sick and old.

Dream big, reach for the stars now.

Not long after Amazon published this book review online, a curmudgeon commented about my review with an unforgiving critique of the book. I'll refer to him here as "David: The Troll." Here's what he wrote:

> *Part of determining a book's value is looking at whether it has staying power. That is, does it pass the test of time or was it just the "flavor of the day." Books with something worth saying continue to have an impact long after their first publication and you see that reflected in sales. After reading his thoughts and the glowing reviews, I thought that a book which was filled with trite statements worthy at best of a poorly written greeting card would eventually fall from notice. There was nothing of any real substance to the book or to Pausch himself who lived a life of privilege in a greenhouse environment far away from the vicissitudes of daily life. It turns out that I was right. You can now purchase online from various retailers the hardbound version for ninety-nine cents in very good condition. New editions are just a few dollars more. Of course, the people who praised Pausch have probably moved on to someone else who tickles their ears and eyes with thoughts that never go beyond the surface. Decades from now, I suspect that social historians will use this book as an example to paint our times as one in which people wanted easy answers not necessarily true ones.*

Well, you'll understand that I did not accept David: The Troll's critique without a rebuttal. So here is my comeback:

Dear David:

If Randy Pausch's grave was near your home, would you also dance on it?

You have missed the central purpose of the book. He didn't write the book for you, nor did he write it for me, nor for the millions who have purchased copies. He wrote it for his children. If you had watched his Last Lecture on YouTube, you'd know this. It was his central point at the conclusion of the lecture.

Fortunately, Randy went to his grave feeling the sublime satisfaction that he had made a difference and left something behind of significance. Frankly, every good man and woman deserve an equivalent sense of closure at death's door.

The book was adjunct to the lecture and probably would not have become a priority if he had not become famous in a matter of weeks, and thus a market opportunity appeared, no doubt propelled by his co-author Jeffrey Zaslow. Fortunately, Randy did not have to suffer the slings and arrows of latter-day critics such as you.

All I see in your comments is the rumblings of a jealous person who has little better to do than tarnish the image of a dead man who gave his final months answering the needs of millions, helping them find other perspectives on how to die with purpose and dignity ... how to propel oneself into the future of children ... then grandchildren ... and great-grandchildren.

What will you leave behind that will even come close to the final incandescent months of Randy Pausch? You apparently cannot contemplate how Randy's single death has helped nudge the social and cultural narratives around dying and death. But it has.

For the record, I can purchase all great literary classics for cents on the dollar, if not from Amazon, then at secondhand bookstores. Price is but one measure of value, and you cannot possibly know how The Last Lecture has impacted those who have recently lost or soon will lose loved ones. You cannot know how many his story influenced to write a memoir or record a video for their descendants or even simply appreciate their children a little more.

Undaunted and outraged, David: The Troll, fired back:

No. I would not dance on Pausch's grave, but I would pity him as I do those of you who think there's anything of significance in his book. Given your background in marketing, I'm not surprised at how you assume various things about me which have no basis in reality. For example, I did watch the entire video. I also know as well that the book was intended for his kids. However, it grew far beyond that. Of course, his kids might have appreciated it more if he had spent the time with them instead of writing a book but that was Pausch's choice. I think it was the wrong choice save that it left his family financially secure. Even so, let me point out that Pausch would not have needed to do that if he had done the sensible thing and purchased sufficient life insurance once he took on the responsibility of a family. But, that's just another example of how Pausch was pretty clueless about real life. If no one challenged Randy personally about what he wrote in the book while he was alive, then that's sad. Pausch may have gone to his grave satisfied, but it was the satisfaction one gains from ignorance.

Do you really want to get into a contest as to whether Randy Pausch or I will leave a more lasting heritage? For all your words of praise, his book after only a few years is relegated to the bargain book bin. I have more than a few years of experience in the business of selling books. When you can sell new editions for just a few dollars, then that book is long past its heyday and on its way out. But, don't let facts get in the way of your hero worship. Also, there are people including children who are alive today because I put my life on the line for them. My financial situation was also whacked big time because I defended those who needed my help. That's satisfaction enough for me even if it isn't for you.

Lastly, you make the comment that I cannot possibly know many things. However, I do know that I have had far more experience with the ups and downs of life than Pausch ever did and that my ideas were tested in the crucible of crisis instead of the comfortable cocoon that encompassed his life. Life demands more than a set of trite and even untrue sentiments that would be best suited for marketing posters and greeting cards.

After David: The Troll's second fusillade, I decided to allow him the last word about *The Last Lecture* and move on. He is clearly an angry man, probably dispirited about his life, and possibly feeling that he has not received the attention and credit he deserves. He seems unwilling to appreciate the spiritual context of Randy's final gifts to his children: a compelling YouTube video and a small book entitled *The Last Lecture*. Previously I wrote about lessons I received from my father, and those experiences were almost always packaged as simple aphorisms, often fatherly clichés that I did not fully appreciate when they were first uttered. That did not take away from the enduring power of those lessons in my life. I believe Randy's children, as well as other readers ready to receive his parting counsel, will see much deeper into the meaning and implications of his simple ideas and accessible stories.

As I thought more reflectively about Randy's achievement, his deployment of contemporary digital communication tools to spread his thoughts and ideas to millions, I reacted by writing an essay about how any human today can potentially propel himself or herself into the distant future, a powerful potentiality to help transform the ultimate loss of ourselves at death into longevity.

THE IMMORTALITY NARRATIVE

When we depart this life, must the stories of our existence fade within the passing of a few years? That has been the fate of billions of mortals who have preceded today's living.

Since the beginning of human history around 50,000 B.C., 108 billion humans have been born. Just over seven billion are living now, or 6.5 percent of all those ever born are still breathing—a tiny fraction when we consider the meteoric growth of world population today.

How much do we know of the 101 billion humans who have preceded us? The majority are nameless, forgotten as if they never lived, merely dust in the wind.

Except for a relative handful of kings, queens, heroes, political leaders, scientists, artists, writers, intellectuals, athletes, and celebrities who have been held in perpetuity through their works or historical documentation by others, the clear majority of human stories have just perished. We know nothing of those masses who have lived and passed on. Most of us do not know anything about the lives and times of our great-great-great grandparents, if even their names.

Five thousand years ago, in Mesopotamia, the ancient lands between the Tigris and Euphrates rivers now called Iraq, something miraculous happened in the evolution of our species and its ceaseless battle against temporality. Humans discovered how to write.

Death could no longer silence people after departing their mortal bodies. The written word gave our species the power to reach through millennia and speak inside the heads of those living in the distant future.

Then something else happened, another miracle of self-preservation. Enheduanna, daughter of the first emperor in history, was also the first person known to sign her name to a literary creation.

She lived 4300 years ago, and her gift to humanity was the possibility of immortality that can be bestowed by the written word when assigned to a single visionary author. The writing was no longer nameless, codified thought but personal ownership in the future.

Enheduanna's name means "Lady Ornament of the Sky." For centuries after her death, the first author continued to set standards for culture, literature, liturgy hymns, poetry, and religion. Her legacy includes an extensive body of creative output, including forty-two poems, psalms, and prayers that have served as a template for poets, priests, and scribes throughout history.

We know that she existed at a certain point in time. We know what she dreamed. We are aware of her fearlessness and prescience. We know she was a great author, composer, poet, and High Priestess of the ancient Moon God Nanna at temples in the Mesopotamian city-states of Ur and Uruk (Iraq).

Enheduanna lives today, four-and-a-third millennia after she exhaled her final breath. She speaks to us through her creations—and when combined into a complete archive, we have her time capsule filled with revelations that we can contemplate at will.

A generation ago most unexceptional people, removed from the public eye, could not hope to persist beyond death, except perhaps as represented by a deteriorating marker bearing an irrelevant name, lost somewhere in a cemetery or mausoleum. Without notable personal achievements that would become written documents or audio or video recordings, it was not possible for the majority to survive beyond the grave.

With the advent of the digital age and the extraordinary power and memory of the internet, it is now possible for anyone to write and record their thoughts, dreams, and values for others to read, see, and hear—and with archival preservation, for thousands of years from now. Today, for the first time in human history, anybody can paddle beyond the grave, aiming for the distant shores of time. As has Randy Pausch.

QUESTIONS TO CONTEMPLATE
ABOUT YOUR "LAST LECTURE"

Which of your life lessons are most important to share with your children or other young people in your life?

Have you been inspired by classic children's book characters, and, if so, which characters had the most impact on your views and values?

Who would you most like to attend your last lecture and why are these people most important?

If you were to be diagnosed with a terminal disease, such as pancreatic cancer, how would you prefer to spend your final months of "functional health," if granted this time for closure? What would be your priorities?

What tangible memories about you would you like to leave for future generations, and in what form would these memories be encapsulated? A book or other writing? A video? Artwork?

HOW CAN YOUR GENERATION
INFLUENCE YOUR SPIRITUALITY?

⌒

GENERATIONS CHANGE SOCIAL and cultural realities as experienced by individuals. Karl Mannheim, one of the founding fathers of sociology, observed and documented the concept of generations and how birth cohorts can assert considerable influence on shared values and behaviors.

In my second business book, *Generation Reinvention*, published in 2010, I discuss Mannheim's theories and the impact generations can have on the way we collectively look at our social-cultural context, including spirituality and religiosity, as follows:

Karl Mannheim stimulated the robust field of generational research. In a definitive and pivotal essay "On the Problem of Generations," published first in German, in 1928, and then again in 1952, in English, Mannheim considered the impact of generational experiences on groups across social class and geography. He defined a generation as a group representing "a common location in the historical dimension of the social process."

According to Mannheim, a generation is a group bound together by the historical context in which they were born. This conception recognizes that while human history can be traced through game-changing advancements of technologies, it is also about an evolving social context that determines how individual members participate in their social environment. Mannheim believed that the influence of one's generation could be as powerful as the impact of social class.

Thus, a generation implies membership in a unique group, bound by common history, which eventually develops similar values, a sense of shared history, and collective ways of interpreting experiences as the group progresses through the life course.

But simply being part of a group born during a time in history is not sufficient to create the powerful metavalues that differentiate one generation from another. Generations constitute because of dominant biological imperatives and external environmental circumstances. Some factors are universally true about generational formation; others are more specific to a given generation's unique position in history and whether it develops a ubiquitous sense of itself.

The first factor that determines many of the special qualities of a generation is the impact of "intergenerational continuity." We learn many of our bedrock values as children of older generations. Many values we take for granted as part of our collective American (or Western or European) value set come from older generations, many of whom have long ago passed into history. Their cherished—and some would say, immortal values—have been given to us through lessons shared within stories, reenactments, books, and historical education.

Mannheim called these "appropriated memories," meaning that we appropriate life experiences from older generations as stories and adopt and adapt the lessons and values inherent in these memories. This applies to historical lessons that come to us as children forming early impressions of our place in the larger context.

As children, our brains have not developed neurologically to the extent that we can critically examine major experiences in our lives without looking at our parents and other adults for nuanced interpretation and meaning. We not only experience a major external event at some level of critical awareness; we also construct meaning for the event by "appropriating" meaning from adults in the communities who influence us.

Early in our teen years, biology intersects with sociology. As sexual maturation becomes a significant factor in our lives, our brains also develop sufficient cognitive and emotional processing capabilities to begin acquiring memories; we start interpreting what's happening in our lives from introspection and then providing our own definitions of meaning. But group sociology also becomes a significant factor in our interpretation of these newly "acquired memories."

Mannheim observed that we develop a profound awareness of our position in the social structure as teenagers. Teens become motivated and often manipulated by their primary reference groups. To many, friends become far more important than parents and families.

So as teenagers we experience the same weighty national and international events as do our parents, but because of biological maturation arriving at the same time as an irresistible peer-group focus, we experience "fresh contact." By this Mannheim means that generational consciousness develops, which influences changes in the content of our experiences, leading to "mental and spiritual adjustment." Fresh contact means the new interpretation of experience, modified by our susceptibilities to peer influences.

Mannheim further concludes that acquired memories are far stronger than appropriated memories, which further explains why generations sometimes have great difficulty understanding significant life issues in the same way. A World War II vet experienced the horror of that war, but no amount of reenactment through media will fully engage younger generations not yet born during the war. We may get a sense of the war vicariously through movies and other forms of storytelling, and we may feel empathy for the portrayed characters, but we can never fully understand the full panoply of emotions that spring from that painful chapter of history.

So, another way that Mannheim explains the meaning of "generations" is through the observation that a generation forms when youth experience the same concrete historical problems or events and then members develop a set of "collective strivings leading to a basis of continuing practice."

As we mature into young adults, we transition from reliance on appropriated memories (and the values inherent in those memories) to acquired memories, developing meaning based on personal experiences within the social structure. Our generational affiliation can actually change our emotional reflections about our experiences, leading to "collective strivings," whether that might be vehemently protesting a war (by Boomers over Vietnam) or being inspired by patriotic fervor and joining the fight in a war (by Millennials and a rush to enlist in the military and subsequent fighting in Afghanistan following 9/11).

Another way we can think of generational consciousness is to look at collective mentalities that reflect a dominant view of the world based on individual experiences. These collective evaluations of major events—whether technological, economic, cultural, social, or political—can lead to the formation of similar attitudes and values. These values can foment shared action, whether war protest marches or a rush to enlist.

A significant insight taught by Mannheim is an understanding that "collective mentalities" can become the basis of "continuing practice" or shared action in the future.

Once generational experiences begin to be acquired early in the teen years, generational identification also begins. How much we come to identify with the values of our generation is a personal process, and many within a generation eventually choose to reject some prominent values associated with their birth cohort. A generation that has been known for protesting authority, especially military conscription, also has members that vehemently oppose so-called "peaceniks." A generation understood as dominantly liberal also has outspoken conservative members. A characteristically frugal generation has notable spendthrifts.

The degree of turmoil in the macro-environment during the critical years of generational formation can predict the extent to which a generation has a sense of its identity. Many critics who belong to other generations have lamented that Boomers seem to be an extraordinarily self-absorbed generation, and Boomer culture, whether rock music or fashion, has, to some, a tiresome, dominating influence on mainstream culture. Another way to understand this is to recognize that Boomers came of age as young adults during a time of enormous social and political struggle, from race riots in the main urban centers to conflict over an offensive war in Southeast Asia. This turmoil, in concert with substantive cultural changes propelled by mass media—from the sexual revolution to adoption by men of long hair styles—created a period in history of astonishing and rapid change. American Boomers may have such a strong sense of generational identification because their teen years were characterized by massive upheaval in the world outside their high schools and colleges. Generational thought leaders used media to disseminate "collective mentalities," which became encoded in rock 'n' roll songs and popular art, fashion, and literature.

High levels of generational identification occur when age (in this case, youth) becomes its social category and peers become a powerful, salient reference group. We have positive associations with our peers and negative associations with those outside our group, namely parents and adult authorities of other generations. I believe we can agree that Boomers identified with their youth culture while widely rejecting the cultural norms of older generations.

Boomers embraced shared ideas, dress, music, slogans, symbols, and ways of reacting to perceived dominance by other generations. Boomers became the first generation in modern times to possess such a high degree of self-awareness, which of course media and marketing communities were delighted to reinforce.

One way to describe this phenomenon of generational identification is the concept of a cohort effect, which Mannheim writes about as "the taste, outlook, and spirit characteristic of a period or generation." He also referred to the notion of zeitgeist, the idea that a generation has a collectively shared sense of its formative historical period.[44]

Thus, a theory of generations also points toward the area of spirituality. Generations often view their spiritual and religious lives from very different perspectives; yet, many formal religious traditions transfer from generation to generation through organized religion. Within the boundaries of time-honored religious teachings and practices, however, generations can and do find unique ways of conceptualizing, communicating, and promoting emerging spiritual beliefs and practices. These evolving ideas can take on deep academic explorations, such as the emergence of existential philosophy in mainstream culture during the 1960's. Spiritual beliefs that gain popular recognition and cultural currency can even be found on protest placards, such as:

1. *War is not healthy for children and other living things.*
2. *Make love, not war.*
3. *The most important things in life are not things.*
4. *Silence = Death (concerning the AIDS epidemic)*
5. *The next war will determine not what is right but what is left.*
6. *They also die who stand and watch.*
7. *Wanted: Jesus Christ.*

---

44   Green, Brent, *Generation Reinvention: How Boomers Today Are Changing Business, Marketing, Aging, and the Future*, 2010, published by Brent Green & Associates, Inc.

Applying my understanding of generational sociology, I have written about Baby Boomer spirituality in another book I published in 2006, *Marketing to Leading-Edge Baby Boomers*. This short chapter is germane to questions about how generational affiliation can stimulate a "spiritual zeitgeist," thus inspiring dominant approaches to understanding and experiencing our spiritual lives. Here is my chapter excerpt concerning Boomer spirituality, which I hope will stimulate equivalent contemplation from members of other generations reading this book.

SEEKING SPIRITUAL ANSWERS

I am an eagle. The great rock upon which I perch allows me to see a panorama spanning from the Atlantic Ocean to the western Cascade Mountains. The valley below connects east with west.

Covered by dark green forests and rusty sandstone and often shrouded in mist, my great valley overflows with wandering people. When I soar above them on swirling thermal gusts, I see millions in search of answers to great questions.

They are busy with their lives, and most do not notice me: They look down instead of up.

They are a generation caught up in mid-life; so much possesses them: ebbing careers, fleeing children, declining parents, retirement thoughts, mortality fears, and uncertain times.

They look down, not up.

Wings are wondrous. I slice through the crisp air and soar the span of this, my valley. Time is not an issue because I float relentlessly above so many busy lives, and I pass through their history and future.

I follow the pitter-patter of their lives; I hear anguish; I see loneliness.

This generation does not know itself as well as it once did.

I dive from clouds toward the great yearning below, and just before the collision, I arch my neck, soaring back to the universe above.

In swift seconds, I come to know their emptiness, their earthbound ties, and their yearning for spiritual freedom such as mine.

In 1971, John Lennon asked the world to imagine that there is no heaven through his influential song, "Imagine."

> *Imagine there's no heaven*
> *It's easy if you try*
> *No hell below us*
> *Above us only sky*
> *Imagine all the people*
> *Living for today...*[45]

— JOHN LENNON, *IMAGINE*

The legendary poet-musician bid us to withdraw from the overburdened promises of immortality, embodied and embellished by formal religions; rather, he challenged us to embrace secular spirituality, to honor peace and brotherhood in the present, to eschew the unrealized promise of salvation in a hypothetical afterlife.

His song struck a responsive chord in the hearts of millions, and though it is a rebuke of formal religion to some, to others, it is a powerful call for religiosity: the gathering and honoring of timeless principles embodied in the great religious traditions.

This anthem spoke to seekers of higher spiritual truths, and its simple lyrics resonated with a generation. The timeless ballad from a cultural icon has been etched into the religious glossary of Baby Boomers.

When I hear this song, I recall a campfire setting about ten years ago, and a chance encounter with Jane, a cousin of a long-term business associate. We had gathered at a campsite near the foot of Pikes Peak to enjoy clean fall air and blazing aspens in golden transformation. The camping area filled with the odors of fresh food cooking over a fire and spiritual connections emanated from this primitive gathering.

John Lennon's enigmatic entreaty beckoned from a nearby radio.

---

45   "Imagine," words and music by John Lennon, copyright 1971

Her skin had a weathered patina, much looser and leatherier than her forty-eight years would usually summon. Her skin's permanent walnut shade suggested that she, like so many of her peers, worshiped the sun during the sixties and seventies and had spent many hours of later adult life tending gardens. A bright spark in her gray-blue eyes suggested a continuing need for contact with people and experiences. She had the figure of an adolescent woman: thin, petite, and muscular, with thighs unprovoked by childbearing.

I introduced myself to her at a picnic table shaded by an aspen grove, and somehow, I knew that she was not only a child of the sixties zeitgeist, she was also a woman in search of new meaning.

We talked about food during the first few minutes of this new relationship. She had grown the tomatoes for her salad in a hydroponics garden; the sweet yellow corn was farm fresh. Then the sun set behind us as we prattled on about the healthy fare, and dull gray shadows crossed her beaming face. Something seemed very private about her, haunting, and I sensed deep wells that I needed to probe for insights.

After dinner, we gathered with our friends around a large campfire. The snapping aspen logs created an intimate glow, and so I spoke intimately, without qualification or pretense.

"Our generation needs another spiritual leader," I suggested, almost as if a test. "We need someone who will pinpoint our collective feelings and better articulate our quest for the remaining years of our lives."

Jane sat quietly on the other side of the fire and listened without challenging. I saw through the tapestry of soft light, and then into the shadows, and I sensed shades of disagreement in those riveting eyes. Her head cocked as if to listen to another, more distant voice.

"This leader needs to be a veteran of the time when we came of age," I continued. "I believe this may come to pass. He or she may rise during a crisis such as economic upheaval, war, or an environmental calamity. But whatever the precipitating event or events, this person will come forward at a time when Boomers will be most receptive to a reexamination

of our deep-seated spiritual quest. Think of this person as our generation's Billy Graham."

Jane looked at me curiously. "I'm not sure that we need a leader. I am
trying to break from a commune right now. They've controlled my life
and wasted twenty years…"

"This leader will not take away our free will," I argued, "but he will
articulate our collective feelings as have the poet-singers of our time."

She looked at me with further suspicion, so I pressed my argument.
"Consider Mahatma Gandhi, for example. He did not tell the Indian
people how to act or feel. He simply modeled and articulated a doctrine
of peaceful resistance and ethnic pride. This is the type of leader that
I'm referring to."

"Why do we need any more leaders? JFK, RFK, and Martin Luther
King have been dead a long time."

I paused and studied Jane's distant gaze but persisted. "Because we
have become fragmented as a generation. We need a collective spiritual
purpose. We often lack a sense of community."

Jane folded her knees up under her chin and grasped her ankles,
almost as if she was becoming a fetus. "Isn't it possible that there is a
collective force, perhaps a consciousness, with which we are all in touch?
And whatever is happening to this generation is going on around camp-
fires like these—where people are turning to each other and talking?"

I sensed her fragility, the lost years spent following a charismatic
leader who proved to be a false profit.

"I remember how free we felt," she confessed. "I mean, I would grab a
backpack and just stick my thumb out…travel anywhere. People weren't
as they are now. It isn't even safe for me to lie beside a stream in the forest, where I feel closest to God. You can't do that anymore. It's often not
safe, to be honest."

Suddenly I saw a delicate soul sitting in the plastic lawn chair—
someone fragile and still innocent in some ways; someone disillusioned
and bitter in other respects. Jane was so much in need of safety and
comfort—call it a yearning for soul petting.

Brad, her husband, pulled her close, and he stared at me through the dancing flames as if I was speaking words that he and she needed to hear.

"That's what I feel," I whispered. "We need a spiritual leader to awaken meaning for a sleeping generation."

Jane squinted through the dancing flames. "Maybe it's all of us finally reaching inside and only manifesting what matters."

Jane's cautious revelations about her deepest feelings, at that time imparted to an argumentative stranger, pointed backward to a time of spiritual starvation when Baby Boomers feasted at an international buffet for alternative spiritual quests: Transcendental Meditation, Gestalt Psychology, Scientology, the Human Potential Movement, Existential Psychology, and the New Age Movement.

For those who succumbed to the excesses of psychoactive substances and only found emptiness, there came the 12-step programs for alcohol, cocaine, and barbiturate addicts.

This cornucopia of spirituality provided a diverse array of choices upon which to carve a meaningful and relevant life. Nevertheless, excesses sometimes overwhelmed revelations.

The creation of community, driven by the yearning for meaning, the affirmation of a worthwhile life in the face of alienation—this is the unfinished business of a generation. The quest is inherently spiritual, and it is becoming a pressing priority.

As freedom from work pressures fill days with time for greater soul-searching, into this vortex will likely flow an elder culture reflecting some of the sixties spiritual culture. Jane's uncertainty, and that shared by her cohort, will find new sources of enlightenment and significance.

Boomers are seekers, and the search intensifies during the next twenty years.

In *A Generation of Seekers*, a seminal book about the spiritual quest of Baby Boomers, Professor Wade Clark Root analyzes many underlying, spiritually-rooted motivations: the importance of experience over beliefs, distrust of institutions and leaders, the universal urge for personal fulfillment, and a yearning for intergenerational community.

Professor Clark also underscores how core values set up a distinctive brand of spirituality that typifies a wide swath of the generation.

1. Acceptance of different lifestyles and cultural traditions;
2. A sense of personal responsibility for life experiences and results;
3. An enduring belief that strength comes from within, and dogmatic adherence to traditional religious prescriptions will not bestow emotional potency;
4. A revealing attraction to self-disclosure, the willingness to share feelings openly in the face of reprisal

A growing percentage of the generation seems to be following John Lennon's enjoinder by casting aside traditional religion for spirituality, a spirituality grounded in temporal meaning and a life-value perspective. There is an acronym gaining currency to describe this major sociological trend: SBNR, meaning *Spiritual but Not Religious*.

This macro trend has created a new spiritual lexicon dominated by such words as quest, journey, growth, searching, choice, exploration, transformation, mindfulness, reinvention, and integration. Of their spiritual searching, Boomers ask for answers to enduring existential questions; insights rooted in direct experience, integration of body and mind, an egalitarian view of religious expression, and emotional ascendance through strengthening community.

Many in the generation are relativistic in their quest, willing to reach into the realm of many divine resources, from ancient Buddhism to cutting-edge cosmology, from crosses to quarks.

This searching culture has generated a marketplace of new spiritual resources, including books, videotapes, audiotapes, weekend retreats, newsletters, Institutes, webinars, and digital networks. Spiritual leaders enter this fray, espousing eclectic paths to transcendence, drawing upon timeworn religious traditions and New Age psychobabble.

Boomers can be characterized as seekers of religious and spiritual pluralism. For many in this cohort—all but the most religiously dogmatic—the path to salvation has few conceptual barriers.

Second, spiritual concerns have, at their roots, a collective desire for community, abundant health, brightening horizons, and, ultimately, life satisfaction. As previously mentioned, there is an underlying search for holistic solutions, those modalities that join body, mind, and spirit.

Finally, spirituality is the wellspring of character and an integrated awareness of the inner self.

The questions Boomers are asking are of temporal proportion, nonetheless as wrenching as what happens after the end of life:

Who will care for me?

Will I be able to provide for my family?

Who am I?

Where am I going?

Could there be more to life than this?

Answer these questions within a spiritual context, and this generation will listen. However, do not foist counterfeit witness, embellished with promises of happiness, or cast down aggressive appeals to belief authority.

Jane, a sixties' and seventies' veteran of false spiritual control, will not listen, and neither will most of her generation.[46]

Perhaps no symbol has had more impact on a collective sense of contemporary spiritual priorities than the peace symbol. It is a symbol of staying power, one graphic icon from the 1960s that will probably be called upon during times of social strife for generations to come. Several years ago, I took the time to explore the history of this arresting symbol, and I share my discoveries here further to amplify the correlations between social and spiritual history.

A GENERATION'S SPIRITUAL ICON: THE PEACE SYMBOL

If you would conduct a worldwide opinion survey to discover one wish for the future of humanity shared across societies and cultures, the chances

---

46 Green, Brent, *Marketing to Leading-Edge Baby Boomers*, Chapter 38, "Seeking Spiritual Answers," Copyright 2005 and 2006, published by Paramount Market Publishing

are that universal yearning would be for peace. The world without war and strife, without sectarian violence, without the omnipresent threat of terrorism—certainly these yearnings are among our most cherished but unrequited dreams.

Boomers attached themselves to this idealistic quest early in their adult lives. Some demonstrated for peace. Some molded lifestyles eschewing violence, whether through nonviolent civil disobedience or conscientious objection to military service. Some sought to influence national war policies through political engagement. Some joined the military to fight for long-term peace. Some joined the military as clergy or nurses. The yearning for peace became the theme of many rock 'n' roll folk songs, with these lyrics among the noteworthy:

Where have all the young men gone?
Long time passing
Where have all the young men gone?
Long time ago
Where have all the young men gone?
Gone for soldiers every one
When will they ever learn?
When will they ever learn?

Where have all the soldiers gone?
Long time passing
Where have all the soldiers gone?
Long time ago
Where have all the soldiers gone?
Gone to graveyards every one
When will they ever learn?
When will they ever learn?[47]

— PETE SEEGER, *Where Have All the Flowers Gone?*

---

47 Seeger, Pete, "Where Have All the Flowers Gone?" words and music by Pete Seeger, copyright 1961

For this generation, peace became a preoccupation.

And one icon subsumed their hopes for a better future: the peace symbol. The graphic image tapped into a collective set of values emerging during a generation's youth, from antiauthoritarian attitudes to youthful thoughts of a more utopian society. To some, it took on inspirational import about moral values like symbols of the world's great religions.

With its growing emotional and motivational subtext, the peace symbol eventually became a useful selling tool as businesses refined modern marketing techniques to create a Boomer revolution in product sales. Marketers quickly recognized the strategic value of co-opting the symbol for product positioning. So-called "head shops" filled initial consumer demand by offering peace symbols as stained glass sun catchers, silver necklaces, refrigerator magnets, tie-dyed T-shirts, and myriad posters. Eventually so did K-Mart and Wal-Mart.

On April 4, 2008, the peace symbol turned 50. The story about how it has become one of the most recognizable symbols of the Boomer generation is significant.

In the spring of 1958, Gerald Holtom, a textile designer and graphic artist from Great Britain, set out to create a mark that could be used at protest events pressing for nuclear disarmament. In perhaps one of the most inspired days of identity design during the 20th century, the artist brought together semaphore symbols for N and D, surrounded by a circle representing the globe. On April 4th, five-thousand people gathered at Trafalgar Square in London to support the "Ban the Bomb" movement and to protest testing and stockpiling of fissionable materials by the world's largest industrial powers. It was on this day that Holtom's memorable icon made its debut.

Protestors walked a few miles from the Square to Aldermaston, location of an atomic weapons research facility. Their placards carried the succinct message of protest in this new and undefined symbol. It needed no explanation, whether viewers understood the symbolic implications or not. Reactions were not always positive; some saw the devil in the logo.

The peace symbol quickly spread to other protest movements representing opposition to the Vietnam War, the quest for racial civil rights, a growing outcry against environmental degradation, and spirited marches for gender and sexual equality. The symbol persisted through Vietnam and onward into the debates about wars in Iraq and elsewhere.

The peace symbol received overdue commemoration in a book published in April 2008 by the National Geographic Society, *PEACE: The Biography of a Symbol*. Author Ken Kolsbun observed that the symbol "continues to exert almost hypnotic appeal. It's become a rallying cry for virtually any group working for social change."

QUESTIONS TO ASK ABOUT YOUR GENERATION'S INFLUENCE ON YOUR SPIRITUALITY

What are the most important religious and spiritual values that you share with your parents?

What are some of the most critical historical experiences in your life that occurred from your mid-teens to your mid-twenties, experiences that have influenced your spiritual attitudes and values today?

Since your early- to mid-20s, what national and international events have had the most profound impact on the way you view your spiritual values and attitudes today?

Thinking back to how you looked at things ten years ago, how have your religious values and attitudes changed when compared with how you feel now?

Imagining how things might change for you in the future, say ten years from now, and based on what you know today, what do you expect to change in your spiritual values, attitudes, and priorities?

HOW SMALL ARE WE?

I ENJOY THINKING about cosmological concepts, the vastness of outer space and our relative insignificance within the unfathomable expanse of the universe and infinite time. This thought process might seem odd, but somehow, sometimes, my thoughts about the human condition and spirituality include a combination of intellectual curiosity and unrestrained astonishment that we even exist.

Noble Prize nominee Andre Malraux declared that "the greatest mystery is not that we have been flung at random between the profusion of the earth and the galaxy of the stars, but that in this prison we can fashion images of ourselves sufficiently powerful to deny our nothingness."[48] Those images of ourselves include our understanding today of humanity's place in the vastness of the cosmos and the immensity of cosmic time.

Human enlightenment began four-hundred years ago, when Roman Catholic orthodoxy ruled the lives of people living at that time. One did not safely question this received authority, and thus those who began to look objectively and curiously at the stars and heavens above sometimes came into conflict with church doctrine. Sacrosanct in church orthodoxy was a decree that the earth dominated the cosmos at the epicenter of the universe, and the sun, planets, and stars circled the earth in humble obedience.

Giordano Bruno (1548—1600), born Filippo Bruno, spent his varied career as an Italian Dominican friar, philosopher, poet, mathematician, and astrologer. An intellectually gifted Renaissance man,

---

48 Malraux, Andre, *The Walnut Trees of Altenburg,* 74

he is illustrious today for his cosmological theories, which went even further than the then-novel and controversial Copernican model. He proposed that the stars were just distant suns surrounded by their own exoplanets, and he dangerously raised the possibility that these planets could even foster life of their own, a philosophical position known as *cosmic pluralism*. That didn't work well for his monotheistic, earth-centric employers. He also insisted that the universe is infinite and could have no celestial body at its center. He had no direct evidence of this, of course, because the cosmological tools and technologies did not then exist, but he had sharp intuitive instincts that compelled him to challenge orthodoxy. He had hoped that his suppositions would be embraced by Rome because this cosmological perspective, he thought, made humanity's place in the universe even more unique and majestic.

Beginning in 1593, the Roman Inquisition prosecuted Bruno for heresy on charges including denial of several core Catholic doctrines. His ignorant contemporaries reviled Bruno's intellectual independence. They were offended by Bruno's rejection of a core Catholic belief that humans are God's children, made in His image, and thus occupy an exalted place in the universe, *living on a planet at the center of everything.* The Inquisition found him guilty, and in 1600 he was burned at the stake in Rome's Campo de' Fiori.[49]

After his death, he gained fame, being celebrated by 19th- and early 20th-century commentators who regarded him as a martyr for the scientific method. Science historians view Bruno's case as a landmark in the history of free thought and the emerging sciences. Bruno's dedication to discovering the truths of existence became "one giant leap for mankind," as he gave his life while insisting that theory must fit observations rather than visa-versa, a core principle of the scientific method and fundamental to our technological civilization today.

---

49 Podcast # 6, Riding the Wave of History: reasonably. live, https://reasonably. live/2016/03/26/riding-the-wave/ (accessed July 20, 2016).

Our intellectual understanding of humanity's place in the cosmos has come a long way since Rome cremated Bruno alive. Some of what we have learned is almost incomprehensible when considered from the perspective of our short lives and small stature before nature's grandeur. Reinhold Niebuhr (1892—1971), an American theologian and professor at Union Theological Seminary for thirty years, looked toward faith to comprehend our small stature in the universe: "O Lord, you have made us very small, and we bring our years to an end like a tale that is told; help us remember that beyond our brief day is the eternity of your love."[50]

How small are we? We are all really, *really small*. Let me explain.

The average adult human weighs about 170 lbs. Earth weighs about 6.58 sextillion tons. Our home planet is relatively massive.

But the Earth is *really small*.

Consider Jupiter, the fifth planet from the sun, a "gas giant" two and a half times more massive than all the other planets in the solar system combined.[51] 1,321 Earths could fit into Jupiter, the largest planet in the solar system.

How about the sun, our solar radiator? 1.3 million Earths could fit inside the sun if you could melt the Earth and pour the liquid into the sun. But if you tried to fill the sun simply with Earth-size balls, you could fit merely 960,000 Earths within the sun's boundaries.

But the sun is *really small*!

One of the stars in the Milky Way Galaxy, a red giant, is called UY Scuti, and you could put 1,900 of our suns inside this monster star.

But UY Scuti is *really small*.

The Milky Way Galaxy has 100 billion stars. It takes 100,000 years for light to travel from one end of the galaxy to the other. You may recall from high school physics that light travels at 186,000 miles per second.

But the Milky Way is *really small*.

---

50 Niebuhr, Reinhold, "The Eternity of God's Love," as quoted on BeliefNet.com: https://goo.gl/Ut8QFX

51 Jupiter Facts - Interesting Facts about Planet Jupiter, http://space-facts.com/jupiter/ (accessed July 20, 2016).

It's part of what's called the "Local Group," which consists of 54 galaxies. The Milky Way and the Andromeda galaxies are the largest. Andromeda is merely 28 light years away from earth. But it takes light 10 million years to travel the diameter of the Local Group.

But the Local Group is *really small.*

The Local Group is part of the Virgo Super Cluster, which has more than one million galaxies. It takes light 110 million years to travel across the Virgo Super Cluster.

But the Virgo Super Cluster is *really small.*

That's because there are an estimated 100 billion galaxies in the universe. It would take 92 billion years for light to cross the observable universe, but the universe is expanding so even at light speed we can never reach the other side.

But our universe is *really small.*

Many esteemed theoretical physicists believe that there is what's called the "multiverse" or multiple universes. And the number of them, according to theory—let's just conclude it is humongous.

When you consider how small we are, you also must consider our size in relationship to time. Neil deGrasse Tyson, the eminent astrophysicist, cosmologist, director of the Hayden Planetarium in New York City, and celebrity spokesman for the reboot of the television series *Cosmos*, demonstrated our smallness in time by putting the entire history of our universe into the context of a single calendar year. This is called the "cosmic calendar."

So, the universe began a nanosecond after midnight on January 1st, and it was *really small*, about the size of one atom. The Big Bang occurred 13.8 billion years ago. The Milky Way galaxy formed March 16th on this cosmic calendar. The oldest rocks on earth formed on September 6th. December 5th introduced the first multicellular life. Primates, our biological ancestors, did not make the scene until December 30th. On this compressed cosmic calendar, all recorded human history, everything our species has encoded through art, stories, inventions, and writing— the entire history of progress—has occurred in the final second of the cosmic year—one second before midnight on December 31st. Relative to the history of time, our existence as a species occupies a *really small* span of time.

But wait, perhaps there is another way to think about our place in the vastness of the cosmos that surrounds this tiny planet. Let's look at this in a different way. There are 37.2 trillion cells in the human body. But the universe has 100 billion galaxies, so each of us is made up of more cells than there are galaxies by a factor of 372.

And consider our brains, at three pounds they are *really small* compared to our body weight—about 2 percent. Our brains consist of 100 billion neurons. Thus, we have as many neurons in our brains as there are stars in the Milky Way galaxy and galaxies in the known universe. And our collective minds have been capable within a span of one second of the cosmic calendar to understand much about the enormity of the universe around us and even create amazing technologies such as an iPhone, the Internet, and screaming fast personal computers. We have traveled to the moon, and through our celestial robots have left the boundaries of our sun's solar system.

We are little specs of organic life with knowledge now accumulating at an exponential rate. We are creating, learning, and inventing more than at any time in human history. This century will not involve 100 years of progress; relative to all human history, the 21st century will involve more than 20,000 years of progress.

We are *really small* in physical size and across the span of all time, but we collectively constitute the largest consciousness in the known universe. So, this makes us tall after all. This also makes our short but impactful human lives consequential. We have the technological prowess to both create and destroy the future.

Neil deGrasse Tyson addresses our smallness and fragility within the context of a vast cosmos:

"If your ego starts out, 'I am important, I am big, I am special,' you're in for some disappointments when you look around at what we've discovered about the universe. No, you're not big. No, you're not. You're small in time and space. And you have this frail vessel called the human body that's limited on Earth."[52]

How does this inquiry into the cosmological facts of space and time relate to loss? My answer is inherently personal but hopefully helpful to your thinking also.

Understanding as much as I can about the dimensions of the cosmos and grand arc of time helps me appreciate the beauty and wonder of human existence and our accelerating comprehension of reality. What was once unfathomable to ancient humans and later denied as religious heresy during the Middle Ages can today be comprehended and explained. We are *really small*, but our enormous collective consciousness has discovered, revealed, dissected, analyzed, and exploited many secrets hidden from our species until less than 500 years ago—not even a fraction of a second of the last minute of the final day of the cosmic calendar. Much of what I've shared in this chapter involves knowledge gained within the last 100 years, although our species has been gazing up at and wondering about the night sky since our ancestors stood on two legs and peered across the savannahs of Africa, even long before our species dwelled in caves.

Among the greatest human minds to have ever lived and died, Albert Einstein appreciated the significance of our unique place in space and time and the planetary caretaking challenges confronting humanity:

A human being is a part of the whole, called by us Universe, a part limited in time and space. He experiences himself, his thoughts and feelings as something separated from the rest—a kind of optical delusion of his consciousness. This delusion is a kind of prison, restricting us to our personal desires and to affection for a few persons nearest to us. Our task must be to become free from this prison by widening our circle of compassion

---

52   deGrasse Tyson, Neil, as quoted on Brainyquotes.com: https://goo.gl/CC0yIv

to embrace all living creatures and the whole of nature in its beauty.[53]

We have lost over 101 billion people through all recorded history. Nevertheless, we have benefited from accumulation and application of their knowledge and technological prowess, arriving here in our time through many sacrifices and much pain and suffering—*their losses*. I repeat: our technical proficiencies and modern mastery over earth's environment can be attributed to an accrual of human losses across 55,000 years. We are who we are now *because of loss*. We have lost tens of billions of humans who have preceded us, and yet we have gained vast intellectual storehouses filled with their knowledge and expertise, often acquired and amplified *through loss*.

This correlation between loss and gain seems equally valid with all that's significant in our individual lives: each of us has lost loved ones, but we have gained from our dearly departed in ways we might not fully appreciate until we ask questions and search for answers. Each of us has lost other nonhuman things we valued: employment, social status, pets, material possessions, and even personality qualities such as self-confidence. Every loss can reveal compensatory gains: productive career transitions, newer social networks that are better aligned with our personalities, higher quality material possessions, a new puppy or kitten, and greater self-assurance in the social sphere. Thus, with every loss comes potential for gain when we think expansively, perhaps gazing upward at the cosmos for inspiration and wonder.

We are human: we lose; we gain; we lose; we gain, and so on.

When considering the befuddling immensity of space and time, and objectively my very small place within all this enormity, I discover perspective and peace. I find comfort knowing that my living body comes from chemical elements set free by catastrophic explosions of stars at the end of their lives—supernovas—ejecting their thermonuclear contents into the cosmos eons ago, eventually forming a tiny blue and breathing

---

53 Ibid., Einstein, SimpletoRemember.com

planet, lively with life, buzzing with monarch butterflies and 8.7 million other species, great and small.

I find comfort knowing that the "star stuff" that is me someday will return to the cosmos as oxygen, carbon, hydrogen, nitrogen, calcium, phosphorous, potassium, sulfur, sodium, chlorine, and magnesium—the elements of life—this single life of mine. I can leave behind some humble contributions to the immense warehouse of accumulating human knowledge. Perhaps the loss of me will become a gain for others in the future.

I find comfort knowing that this elemental sense of reality has another dimension that is spiritual and transcendent. Albert Einstein believed this also: "Everyone who is seriously involved in the pursuit of science becomes convinced that a spirit is manifest in the laws of the Universe—a spirit vastly superior to that of man, and one in the face of which we with our modest powers must feel humble."[54]

An expansive, cosmological awareness helps me appreciate humility and embrace Reinhold Niebuhr's thoughtful meditation, *The Serenity Prayer*:

God, give me the grace to accept with serenity
the things that cannot be changed,
Courage to change the things
which should be changed,
and the Wisdom to distinguish
the one from the other.

Like all of us, I cannot always change the circumstances that bring loss into my life, just as I cannot change the brevity of my life in an astonishing context of 13.8 billion years. Nor can I change the infinitesimal place I occupy on a tiny planet rotating around an average star in a galaxy made up of 100 billion stars and within a universe populated by 100 billion galaxies. Sir Francis Bacon (1561—1626) poetically understood

---

54 Ibid., Einstein, SimpletoRemember.com

the insistence of brevity and the imperative of now: "Begin doing what you want to do now. We are not living in eternity. We have only this moment, sparkling like a star in our hand-and melting like a snowflake…"[55]

Outside the fragility of my existence, there is a divine force greater than I am, and that power includes the combined legacy of billions of humans across 55 millennia. That force includes the gift of my opportunity to contribute to this accumulating human legacy.

I am also comforted by another mature realization: what we lose may not matter as much with psychological distance. Elizabeth Bishop (1911—1979), a Pulitzer Prize-winning American poet and short-story writer, found peace when confronting loss by recognizing that many possessions seem to disappear from our lives because of incomprehensible, mystical, and spiritual intention. Memorably she wrote: "The art of losing isn't hard to master. So many things seem to be filled with the intent to be lost, that their loss is no disaster."[56]

I am on a journey to understand everything I can about the nature of loss, learning what I can change and what I cannot. Within these boundaries, I *choose* to help others understand and accept loss. I *choose* to help us move forward together into the future with greater serenity, more capable of shouldering losses that assuredly will come with passing time.

Finally, I choose to be humble before the forces and dimensions of Nature I can never fully understand. Albert Einstein, the greatest mind to ever comprehend what humans physiologically cannot see, also marveled at this. "What I see in Nature is a magnificent structure that we can comprehend only very imperfectly," wrote Einstein, "and that must fill a thinking person with a feeling of humility. This is a genuinely religious feeling that has nothing to do with mysticism."[57]

---

55 Bacon, Sir Frances, as quoted on GoodReads.com: https://goo.gl/0weR8H

56 Bishop, Elizabeth, The Complete Poems 1927-1979, published by Farrar, Straus & Giroux, Inc. Copyright © 1979, from the poem *One Art*, https://www.poets.org/poetsorg/poem/one-art

57 Ibid., Einstein, SimpletoRemember.com

I hope before it is all over for me that I have become a stronger shoulder to lean on and wiser about loss. This is what is elemental in the part of me that transcends the elements that have created me. This is my source of grace.

QUESTIONS CONCERNING THE SMALLNESS OF HUMANITY

How do you feel when you think about our human stature in relationship to enormous mass, such as a mountain range or even another planet?

Does the brevity of our lives make you sometimes feel insignificant or inconsequential?

Alternatively, does our human mastery over tools and technologies cause you to appreciate and even feel wonder about our collective accomplishments in such a short span of cosmic history? Why?

How can an incisive understanding of the cosmos make us feel more appreciative and accepting of our mortality?

Do you believe that our species can survive our technological prowess, such as the looming threat of nuclear holocaust? Will we harness our technologies for long-term survival of the species, or will we self-destruct?

AFTERWORD

So now I've reached a conclusion of this exploration for answers to difficult questions, although the quest can never finish. I hope you have discovered some insights along the way, if not definitive answers to your most significant questions about loss. We are connected, you and I, because no matter where we are in the life course; no matter how geographically far apart we live; no matter our socioeconomic status, gender, race, sexual orientation, or ethnicity; no matter our place on the spectrum from ignorance to wisdom, we share one existential human quality that impacts all others: we have and will experience loss. Hopefully, each of us in our unique ways will come to terms with loss so we can live fuller and less troubled lives going forward. I wish you well in your search for answers.

But one more thing...

Many years ago, I experienced a convergence of two transformational forces during a single remarkable day: one internal and the other external. Internally, I felt a sudden rush of awareness of my mortality. This feeling came to me as I ate lunch, an everyday experience of existence that we humans take for granted, like breathing or eliminating waste. I thought about all the food a single person must consume during a lifetime, all its forms, and this routine part of daily life gained new significance and elevated meaning. Within the same timeframe, a childhood friend and I beheld a partial solar eclipse during a walk in the Kansas Flint Hills, and for the first time, I noticed that our shadows had softer second shadows, as if shadow auras. From these two occurrences, one familiar and the other extraordinary, I wrote a short story, a narrative about our mortality and inexorable connection to all the generations that have preceded us and will follow long after we are gone.

As Kerry Livgren, a high school classmate and founding member of the progressive rock supergroup *Kansas*, famously penned:

> *I close my eyes, only for a moment, and the moment's gone*
> *All my dreams pass before my eyes, a curiosity*
> *Dust in the wind*
> *All they are is dust in the wind* [58]

— KERRY LIVGREN, *Dust in the Wind*, performed by *Kansas*

WHEN SHADOWS HAVE AURAS

Slathering whole-grain bread with sweet mayonnaise and throwing on salty ham may not be a gourmet's fare, but when you are seven miles from the nearest kitchen and fifteen miles from the closest convenience store, this everyday sandwich becomes extraordinary. Sitting next to me, Henry gazed at nude elm and maple in a grove where we had taken a break. We had been hiking upstream from a small pond, following a feeble brook to its origination source between flint hills converging above. Quiet surrounded us except for munching.

Isis hunched next to my daypack, head poised on front paws, sleek body motionless, eyes darting between us. Henry flipped a morsel into the air above the German shepherd, and her head jolted, and her jaws snapped, making the sandwich wedge disappear.

Having covered all the latest news at the front end of our hike, we had talked ourselves out. Henry gobbled with gratitude, consuming three ham sandwiches as I ate one. He was not a fussy eater; I keep track of his unguarded enthusiasm for food, a wellspring of inevitable teasing.

---

58 "Dust in the Wind," as performed by Kansas - YouTube, http://www.youtube.com/watch?v=12DeNdF0KPA (accessed July 20, 2016), words and music by Kerry Livgren, copyright 1977

Brisk wind swept branches overhead, avoiding us because we sat underneath a cocoon of tree trunks and diminutive evergreens. A hawk circled in a thermal draft above, and I heard its forlorn screech. Reacting to the call of a predatory animal, Isis jerked her rear paw then let it pull back into cocked position. I shifted on a toppled elm tree that served as our couch.

My sandwich tasted suddenly sour. Chewing vigorously, my attention shifted to an amalgam in my mouth. I became aware of the arbitrary idea of food, the necessity of it, and the certainty that like it or not, we must consume organic matter or extinguish. The pleasurable, habitual act of eating became awkward, a foreign experience.

I glanced at Henry and studied crumbs collecting on his beard. He chomped vigorously, reducing a half sandwich to nothing within four bites. Images grew tangible, and my thoughts transcended: the uncomplicated act of eating became synonymous with our struggle to survive inevitability of birth, growth, decline, and death. Capricious chewing to sustain life became the antithesis of death, and that profound insight-filled me with feelings of futility.

As if sensing a blunt shift in my thinking, Isis lifted her head and stared at me with a curious expression. She squeaked softly, asking a question I could not decipher. Assuming her noise was due to hunger rather than concern, Henry tossed her another treat. The morsel hit the leaf-covered ground in front of her; she sniffed and let it lay.

"Eat it up, girl," he said. He looked at me. "Hope she's not sick. She never refuses a treat."

My face must have betrayed dread. A half-eaten sandwich dangled from my hand. The thought of finishing it made me nauseous.

He said, "Are you all right?"

"Just full I guess—have you had enough?"

"I could eat another, but you brought some granola bars, didn't you?"

I reached into a pocket of the pack and handed him a shiny foil package. Bemused, he took the bar from me, removed the wrapper, and nibbled its edges; his eyes darted over my face.

Sometime in the distant future, people are standing in this grove. Male and female, they, like us, are fragile and mortal. They may not eat ham and whole-grain bread, but they eat cells of other beings. They know not of Henry and me, our penchant for fall and flint hills. It is their autumn day, and they feel robust upon inhaling crisp air; they feel the quiet within; they sense connectedness to earth. Two primitive men and a pet have been gone for centuries; any tangible remnants of our life forms have disappeared: powdery dust in the blustery wind. They are our children's children's children's children's children's children. They know of life, not death. Perhaps a dog walks with them, maybe frisky and happy to follow its nose along an aimless path.

"You seem out of it," said Henry.

Continuing to stare at me as if sensing something, Isis had not eaten the tidbit littering matted elm leaves. "No, I'm fine. Let's go."

Henry reached inside the pack and grabbed another sandwich while settling back on his piece of the tree. "In a few seconds," he said.

Trying to shake my mind of future visions, I measured the distance from where we had come and where we might be going. We were in our late sixties, rushing headlong toward the eighth decade of life.

Thought I: late middle age is a realization, desolation, a long ride from somewhere—coming and going—a full-of-life feeling, bubble-popping dream-burning ember. Middle age is chaos and order, extra hair or not enough, aches and heartaches, too-tight blue jeans and worn teeth crowned with gold. It is authority and empathy and anger, long lost lovers and where-could-they-be friends, boredom, reruns of reruns on television, the same old, same old; it's easy-come-easy-go money, and just a few important people who remain in your life—people you can still trust. It's a now-or-never place where all whimsical childhood, teen-age, and young adult years' form to become a weighty bookend on the left of your life and to the right, off in the future, another bookend pushes back with looming weight of untold stories and inevitable end to all stories. It is chances remaining and sustaining—reality gaining hold against hope of a single slam of the great lottery machine: that fading rescue fantasy. Life at mid-life is conveniently bracketed by years passed and the possibility of fewer years coming. Maybe those future people would be at mid-life when they reach this place of tallgrass solitude.

"What's going on?" Henry said. Isis lifted her head again to study us.

"I'm disconnected from here and now," I whispered, "something is happening to me." I looked skyward, sensing a deepening shift.

Picking up an elm branch, Henry drew circles in a patch of undressed dirt. "What's happening?"

The future people act exuberant from walking among ancient hills, sustained in their dimension. They talk incessantly to each other, but they are tentative. I could feel great mystery looming around them—a phantasm hiding in shadows and loneliness, the mystery of reality calling: a sense of past, present, and future. Humans eat to survive, and our relatives from the future, no matter how blessed with unimaginable technologies and psychological separation from hunting and gathering—they, too, eat to weave a dense fabric of 37 trillion cells making up the human body.

The southern sun broke through dark branches overhead, casting our resting spot in yellow-gray light, reminding me of the power of this moment of a single day out of the many that had led to the full expression of me.

Henry munched on a golden delicious apple, staring expectantly, while a pattern took shape.

I said, "Once we ate strained fruits from jars—mushy stuff squishing over our faces and making us appear stupid. Then we consumed boxes and boxes of overly sweet cereals, fried grains full of air, puffy stuff we still sugared generously."

Henry looked perplexed. "Where is this heading?" He threw the apple core into a gully, and Isis jumped. She trotted toward the gully in pursuit of a misunderstood quarry.

"Or how about smoky grilled steaks roasting on an outdoor grill, hot fat sizzling? Bet your dad cooked them, and you ate them—ate browned fat too."

"So?"

"Maybe you ate lobster or crab occasionally—and those meals became exclamation marks among too-repetitive peanut butter, tuna fish and—ham sandwiches on whole-grain bread."

Henry stood and stretched self-consciously. He said, "Either you're still hungry, or you've flipped out. Let's go higher up so we can check out maximum convergence." Afternoon light dulled against the hills above.

I remained seated. "Think about the succession of soups and stews and chilies made from a mishmash of stuff you've eaten—the sum-total of which could fill fields ready for harvest. Think about all that glop we have eaten to become suspended more than halfway through a lifetime of eating."

"You're deliberating the obvious."

"Don't you see? Eating is a metaphor for the absolute demanding exigencies of living. It's our connection to past and future. People of the future will perform this rite as certainly as our aboriginal ancestors."

"Okay. Let's hike."

"You still don't get where I'm coming from. When you wake up one day, as this day, and your life has dramatically shifted gears again for the umpteenth time, and you must graduate from college, or quit your first job, or know you'll never see again the person you always believed would be your spouse or life-long friend—when you unravel knots of enough years to understand tangles, when you become confident that nothing stays the same, but sometimes things change too slowly—then you see an impermanence in our daily rituals to survive—the arbitrariness of it all. What we take for granted takes on momentous gravity."

Henry stomped his right hiking boot on the ground and studied the hills flaming much too softly in the distance. "What's this have to do with eating?"

"Whether we open thousands of more cans or grow our own, we will eat and eat and eat until we can't eat anymore. We now have less than half a chance to get from here to where we want to be before we stop eating for good."

I closed the pack and threw it over a shoulder. Henry grunted as he heavily pushed a few steps ahead. I glanced up the creek bed toward our destination, but I thought about those who will someday be. They have no connection to us, perceive no clear-cut sense of us—we anonymous ones who came before. We had no connection to 101 billion humans who have already lived and died in the last 55,000 years. We had no knowledge of those who walked this path surrounded by great flint hills—which Native American had camped and eaten dried buffalo meat, or which homesteader fished in the ancient pond behind us.

We are disconnected from our past and future but intrinsically bound by time on either side of now. Food sustains us, carries us forward, but it is an organic carbon-based fuel that loses only a small part of its integrity as it passes through our systems. Like food we pass through the system of Earth, changing it, but without much affecting its integrity over eons. People of the future live, eat, die, pass through this same space at another time, change little, and decompose into oblivion—post-consumer waste. We share nothing and everything with them.

Frisky again, Isis sniffed the sandwich morsel drying in the breeze, ate it and then trotted ahead of us. Henry glanced at me over his shoulder with concern.

"I think you're connecting with mortality," he said.

"Perhaps—but it's more than just bad-ass death fears looming here now." I pointed to the obvious abeyance in the sun.

"Wow," he said plaintively as if he suddenly understood more than he saw.

"It's more fundamental."

Isis stopped on the trail ahead and stared impassively at us. I envied her uncomplicated view of things. "It's about connections—about our connections to the past and the future—our ephemeral place between that which has been consumed and that which shall be. Someone in the future will eat molecules known now as Henry. Perhaps those molecules will then be pig or wheat, but Henry will serve a temporal function by helping those mortals defend their fragile grasp of life. Those who came before us now do the same for us. We are of them, and they pass through us to fuel the cycle again."

"Cycles," Henry said flatly. He pulled at his beard and stomped hard on a dead branch to break it. He looked skyward as if to check the time of day by the position of the sun. He squinted at the shift above but appeared reluctant to comment about the obvious.

He saw the manifestation as I did. A partial solar eclipse had begun at 2:37 p.m. I glanced at my watch to see 2:48 p.m. Perhaps forty percent of the sun had been covered. I noticed a sense of cloudiness on a cloudless horizon.

"Unbelievable," Henry sighed. "Let's go there so we'll get a better view of the landscape." He pointed to the top of a flint hill and without looking at me, he charged up the trail behind Isis.

Pack flung loosely over my shoulder, I followed him along a dry creek bed through the dense woodland of elm and oak and up to the top of a ridge. Although only seventy percent of the sun would be covered during an eclipse at this time and place, the landscape took on a premature softness as if the sun had set twenty minutes earlier, but it was just past the apex, and vast plains rolling away from this hill took on an ashen feeling. Isis, seemingly intimidated by the dissonance between light and time-of-day, held back to let us catch up with her, and at a moment of owner and dog reunion, Henry patted her vigorously. He kneeled gently beside her and cupped his arm around her neck. I walked up to them, feeling intrusive.

Then I saw our shadows cast against packed prairie grass, an image routine and insignificant. Around each of our shadows was a second, softer shadow—an aura. I saw one man's shadow—mine of course—and the mixture of a man and a dog—them, Henry and Isis. And around this solid graphic appeared another, softer shadow perhaps two inches in width. Someone shook the camera. God jerked the picture.

"This is an incredible moment," Henry offered philosophically as his bottomless gaze filled with flint and slate sky.

"Answering our imperative to consume, the moon is consuming the sun," I said. "And it is giving us a shadow of our future possibilities and the aura of the way we were." I pointed to the auras around our shadows to make my point.

"Whew," Henry chided. "You feel this eclipse is a metaphor for existence?"

"Fleeting, old friend, this is the time when shadows have auras."

Henry pulled at his beard assiduously and said, "I never knew that an eclipse did this to shadows. I guess I was always inside working or going to school during other eclipses that have come and gone." He fell to his knees to study the effect. "This means something."

"It's a way of considering existence. Look, we are for a short time, during this unprecedented celestial moment, cast in triplicate. Here we are now, flesh and blood." I reached over and stroked Isis' head, and she smiled, her tongue dangling for a cool breeze. I grabbed my extended arm for effect. "This is now, the consequence of sixty-eight years of eating all that glop I spoke of earlier.

"There is our future." I traced the hard outline of our normal shadows. "That is us nanoseconds from now, our shadows cast upon the earth after sunlight passed into and around our bodies but not through them."

Tracing again around the second shadow—the auras—I added, "There is our past—a remarkable, short-lived double exposure made by a moon passing in front of a sun from light that exploded from the sun eight minutes ago."

Henry's eyes glimmered with awe. He also traced with his index finger the outline of our physical bodies, as I had suggested, then he traced around the solid shadows of us in front of us, then he traced around the softer aura.

"We're here, there, and everywhere," he said. "We are a part of now, part of us is past, and we are food for future generations. They will eat us as we transform into them and they into us. We are always connected to the past and future as we digest here in the present—but, my God, now we can see it!"

"I know this must sound ridiculous," I suggested, "but I'm about ready to try one of those chocolate chip cookies. I owe it to future people who will share this majestically simple view of the natural world. I owe respect to those billions who are part of the past, to continue eating because I still have a chance to transform what remains of them into meaningful thought and significant action—for what years remain for me. Eating is arbitrary, necessary, absurd, but it connects us. Besides, each of us mortals has three to feed."

Reaching into the daypack, I grabbed a handful of broken cookies and said, "Want some?"

Robert G. Ingersoll (1833—1899), an American lawyer, an outspoken agnostic, freethinker, and one of the best orators of his time, had spent his early years denying and mocking God, even though he had been raised in a devoutly Christian household. But then he lost his dear brother. As he stood graveside, he knew he needed a more sophisticated concept of God and the hereafter. So later he proclaimed, "Life is a narrow veil between the cold and barren peaks of two eternities. We strive in vain to look beyond the heights. We cry aloud and the only answer is the echo of our wailing cry. From the voiceless lips of the unreplying dead, there comes no word ... but in the night of death, hope sees a star, and listening love can hear the rustle of a wing."[59]

Next time you marvel at a twinkling star so many lightyears away, or on a rare occasion when you see an aura surrounding your shadow, please also see hope. You are loved, and you are not alone.

---

59 Ingersoll, Robert G., as quoted on goodreads.com: https://goo.gl/RLmMvO

ABOUT THE AUTHOR

BRENT GREEN BEGAN his career as a rehabilitation counselor then transitioned to marketing communications. Today he is a creative director, author, speaker, and trainer specializing in Baby Boomers, the generation born from 1946 through 1964. He solidified his international reputation as a generational expert with *Marketing to Leading-Edge Baby Boomers* (2003, 2006). His most recent nonfiction book is *Generation Reinvention* (2010). A popular speaker focused on Boomers, business and aging, his previous keynotes for the long-term care and hospice industries include the National Hospice Work Group, the New Mexico Association for Home & Hospice Care, and Florida Hospices and Palliative Care. He also provided in-depth commentary for a PBS hospice documentary entitled *Except for Six.*

Made in the USA
Monee, IL
05 December 2020